YOUR ATTITUDE IS SHOWING

A PRIMER OF HUMAN RELATIONS

SIXTH EDITION

Elwood N. Chapman

MACMILLAN PUBLISHING COMPANY
New York

COLLIER MACMILLAN CANADA
Toronto

MAXWELL MACMILLAN INTERNATIONAL
New York   Oxford   Singapore   Sydney

Acknowledgments for art on front and back cover appear on page iv.

Macmillan Publishing Company
866 Third Avenue, New York, New York 10022

Collier Macmillan Canada, Inc.
1200 Eglinton Avenue East, Suite 200
Don Mills, Ontario M3C 3N1

Library of Congress Cataloging-in-Publication Data

Chapman, Elwood N.
   Your attitude is showing: a primer of human relations/Elwood N.
Chapman.–6th ed.
      p.   cm.
   ISBN 0-02-321504-6
      1. Psychology, Industrial.   2. Industrial sociology.
   3. Interpersonal relations.   I. Title.
   HF5548.8.C36   1991
   158.7–dc20
                                                            90-5494
                                                              CIP

Printing: 1 2 3 4 5 6 7 8   Year: 1 2 3 4 5 6 7 8 9 0

PREFACE

The first five editions of *Your Attitude Is Showing* have been used in the classroom and workplace for twenty-six years to train both new and experienced employees. Over one million copies have been distributed. It remains one of the most highly regarded primers in the field of business human relations.

Your Attitude Is Showing has helped individuals of all ages and backgrounds play their human-relations roles with greater understanding and sensitivity. I believe this sixth edition will be equally welcomed by teachers and students, managers and employees, and those who seek self-improvement.

Although the twenty chapters remain basically the same, new material connecting attitude with stress, ethics, and other areas of personality development have been added. At the request of users, more emphasis has been placed upon *service* attitudes.

As you read and study *Your Attitude Is Showing*, keep in mind that people who balance their technical skills with human-relations competencies find greater on-the-job happiness, contribute more to the productivity of organizations and, in general, have more successful, rewarding careers.

For this sixth edition, I am indebted to many reviewers and other users around the country whom I have interviewed. I would also like to thank Philip G. Yuhas and Jeanne Pierotti, two young managers who made a major contribution to this edition.

E. N. C.

ACKNOWLEDGMENTS

The art on the front cover is entitled "70 Years Young." Copyright *Armstrong's* 1983. It is a limited-edition collector plate created by *Armstrong's*, Pomona, California, from an original oil painting by Red Skelton, one of America's favorite clowns. This collector plate is a numbered edition of 15,000, 10½ inches in diameter and banded in gold.

The back cover is entitled "Happy." Copyright *Armstrong's* 1977. It, also, is a limited-edition collector plate created by *Armstrong's*, Pomona, California, from an original oil painting by Red Skelton. This plate is a numbered edition of 10,000, 8½ inches in diameter and banded in gold.

Inquiries regarding these popular collectibles should be directed to Armstrong's, 150 East Third Street, Pomona, California 91766.

The author and publisher sincerely thank Mr. Red Skelton and Mr. David W. Armstrong for allowing us to reproduce the Red Skelton collector plates on the front and back cover of this book.

CONTENTS

PART I UNDERSTANDING YOURSELF   1

Chapter 1   You Can't Escape Human Relations   3
Chapter 2   Human Relations Can Make or Break You   10
Chapter 3   Hold On to Your Positive Attitude   19

PART II RELATIONSHIPS WITH OTHERS   29

Chapter 4   Vertical and Horizontal Working Relationships   31
Chapter 5   Productivity — A Closer Look   40
Chapter 6   The Winning Combination   50
Chapter 7   Your Most Important Working Relationship   58
Chapter 8   Understanding the Nature of Relationships   68
Chapter 9   Releasing Your Frustrations Harmlessly   81
Chapter 10 Restoring Injured Relationships   89

PART III BUILDING YOUR CAREER   97

Chapter 11 Succeeding in a New Job or Assignment   99
Chapter 12 Initiation Rites — Coping with Teasing and
            Testing   108
Chapter 13 Absenteeism and Human Relations   116
Chapter 14 Five Common Human-Relations Mistakes   124
Chapter 15 Business Ethics, Rumors, and the Confidence
            Triangle   134
Chapter 16 Two Routes to the Top   143

Chapter 17   Keeping a Positive Attitude Through Plateau
             Periods and Reorganizations   151
Chapter 18   When You Are Tempted to Scramble   158
Chapter 19   Attitude Renewal   167
Chapter 20   Should You Become a Manager or
             a Leader?   178

Suggested Answers to Case Problems   185

Index   199

CASE PROBLEMS

1. Reality   9
2. Adjustment   17
3. Credit Blues   27
4. Decision   39
5. Message   48
6. Insight   57
7. Choice   67
8. Currency   80
9. Frustration   88
10. Restoration   95

11. Nonprofessional   107
12. Confrontation   115
13. Balance   123
14. Motivation   133
15. Dilemma   142
16. Preference   150
17. Change   157
18. Interview   165
19. Focus   177
20. Sensitivity   184

INTRODUCTION

This book could be appropriately subtitled *Gaining Personal Success in Business*, for nothing has more impact on career success than one's attitude. Illustrations like the one below will help you become more aware of the strong impact your attitude has on every aspect of your life. Each drawing shows an amoeba — a microscopic one-celled creature who is constantly changing in size and shape and who is often referred to as the lowest form of animal life. I hope the little amoeba will act as a reminder that, no matter where you are or what you are doing, *Your Attitude Is Showing*.

"After all, I'm just an amoeba."

PART I

UNDERSTANDING YOURSELF

CHAPTER 1

YOU CAN'T ESCAPE HUMAN RELATIONS

Most employees, even those with considerable experience, greatly underestimate the importance of human relations in building their careers.

They pass it off as nothing more than common sense.

They say it is something that one handles intuitively.

They are blind to the significance of the subject because they wrongly assume they are automatically good at it.

But what exactly is *human relations?*

On the simplest level, human relations is being sociable, courteous, and adaptable. It is avoiding trouble with fellow workers. It is following the rules of simple etiquette. But as important as these qualities are to personal success, they only scratch the surface. Human relations is much more than behaving courteously so that people will like you. There is a second, more complex level.

Human relations is also knowing how to handle difficult problems when they arise. It is learning to work well under demanding and sometimes unfair superiors. It is dealing effectively with conflict. It is understanding yourself and how you communicate with others. It is building and maintaining long-term relationships with family, friends, and co-workers. It is knowing how to restore a working relationship that has deteriorated. It is learning to live with your frustrations without hurting others or jeopardizing your own career. It is communicating the right kind of attitude during an employment interview. It is the foundation upon which good management careers are built. In short, it is *building and maintaining* relationships in many directions, with many kinds of people, in both good and bad working environments.

Positive attitudes appreciated. The most popular and productive people in any work environment are usually those employees with the best attitudes. Their positive attitudes

- inject humor into what otherwise would be just work. Everyone misses these individuals when they are on vacation.

- add to the team spirit by "bonding" everyone together in a more positive and productive mood. Many are unofficial leaders greatly appreciated by supervisors.

- make it easier for co-workers to maintain their upbeat attitudes. This, in turn, helps co-workers maintain productivity and enhance their own careers.

Employees who are consistently negative put an added strain on their co-workers. Their negative attitudes

- make it more difficult for others (especially the supervisor) to stay positive. Everyone operates under a needless handicap.

- act like a spoiled apple in a barrel, causing fellow employees to lose their enthusiasm and motivation to contribute. (Why produce more when Jack or Judy gets by with being so negative?)

- repress the fun and harmless horseplay that would normally surface and make everyone feel better about what they are doing. It often takes many highly positive attitudes to offset one that is negative.

Attitudes travel. When others are making a big effort to remain positive in their work environment, a single negative attitude can act as a "cloud" over the entire atmosphere. Productivity can drop. Customers can be treated poorly. Positive employees may seek opportunities elsewhere. Not everyone can be an attitude "star," but negative attitudes damage human relationships in the workplace. Those who find it difficult to remain positive are invited to concentrate on chapters 3, 17, and 18.

In the business world, human relations (attitude) is viewed best in terms of productivity because productivity is the goal of all group activity. Human relations, of course, is not a substitute for work; it cannot replace or camouflage poor performance. Employees are valued primarily for the amount of work they turn out. Your employer will expect you to do your share of the work load — and if you are interested in moving ahead, you will want to do more than your share. An employer will not be interested for long in an employee who has a great attitude but produces very little.

But getting the work out is only one side of the coin. You should accomplish this work and still be sensitive to the needs of those who work with you. You should perform your work without trying to show up your fellow workers or antagonize them. You should carry your full load in such a way that others will be encouraged to follow rather than reject you.

No matter how ambitious or capable you are, you cannot become the kind of employee you want to be (or the kind of employee management wants you to be) without learning how to work effectively with people. It would be career suicide to join an organization and ignore the people who work around you. You simply cannot escape human relations.

Does this mean that you should deliberately set out to play a game of human relations on your new job? The answer depends upon what you mean by "playing a game."

If you mean that you should play up to those who can do you the most good and pay little attention to others, the answser is, of course, no.

If you mean that you should devise a master strategy that will give you the breaks at the expense of other people, the answer is again no.

If, however, you mean that you should sincerely do everything you can to build strong, friendly, and honest working relationships with *all* the people you work with — other employees and supervisors alike — the answer is an unqualified yes.

Does this come as a shock?

If so, think about it. Working hard is not enough in our modern society. It may have been thirty years ago, but it isn't today. You, as a new or experienced employee, have a definite human-relations role to play.

You can't ignore it.

You can't postpone it.

From the moment you join an organization you assume two responsibilities: (1) to do a job—the *best* job you can do with the work assigned to you—and (2) to get along with *all* the people to the best of your ability. It is the right combination of these two factors that spells success.

Perhaps you are a highly qualified, experienced employee happy in your present work environment. Or perhaps, after working a number of years for a particular company, you are making a mid-life career change. Or you may be graduating from an educational institution soon, and you are preparing to launch your career. The possibilities are endless, but no matter what your personal conditions are now, or what they may be in the future, human relations will play a dominant role.

It would be wrong, of course, to say that the skills or abilities you possess are unimportant. If you are employed as an office manager, your computer competencies are vital. If you are employed as an apprentice machinist, your mechanical ability is important. If you are a registered nurse hoping to get into management, your professional training and background are vital. These skills helped you get where you are, and they will help you make progress.

But they are not enough.

In order to make your education and experience work for you as effectively as possible, you must become competent in human relations. You must learn the technique of working with others.

Why?

Because your behavior has a direct bearing on the efficiency of others. Because your contribution will not always be an individual contribution; it will often be a group effort, and you will only be a part of the group. Because what you accomplish will be in direct proportion to how well you get along with the people who work with you, above you, or for you.

Almost everything you do will have an effect on other people. If the effect is good, people may do a better job. If the effect is bad, they will be less productive. Your personal work effort will not be enough. You should conduct yourself in such a manner that those who work with you and near you will also become effective. As you move into supervisory roles, you will be judged less on your personal productivity and more on the team you manage.

Now let's take a closer look at this word *productivity*. Productivity is a significant word in business, industry, and government today. Every organization is operated either to make a profit or to reach a certain level of excellence.

Management has its own ways of measuring work productivity. Some jobs are more easily measured than others. If you are employed as a factory worker, for example, your productivity would be measured by the amount of work you perform over a certain time.

Some organizations employ time-study experts to measure the time required to perform a given task and to establish standards of performance. As an employee of such a company, you would be expected to exceed this standard. If you are employed in a sales organization, for instance, you might be given a sales quota that you would be expected to reach or exceed.

The point is that everyone's productivity is measured. We must all live up to the standards that prevail in our particular business. There is some form of measurement or evaluation for every job.

However, our value is measured not only by the actual work we do, but also by the contribution we make to the department as a whole. This is human relations — as management sees it. Productivity is not only an individual matter, it is also a divisional or department matter. For management has discovered that the way in which people get along together has a great deal to do with departmental productivity.

Let us take the example of a checker in a supermarket. The productivity of a checker is usually measured in three ways: speed, accuracy, and relations with customers. But it doesn't stop there. Why? Because the way others react to her (or him) has an influence on their own productivity, as well as on the productivity of the checker. If she is an excellent checker and measures above others in all three categories, one would think she would be the best checker of all. But would she? Not necessarily.

Let us assume that it is a peak period in the supermarket and all checkers are extremely busy. Shoppers are lined up in front of each checkstand. One of the other checkers suddenly runs out of paper sacks and calls for our "superior" checker to toss him a few. What if our checker says, "Come and get 'em if you want 'em." What would happen? A psychological barrier would immediately arise between the two checkers. The checker requesting the bags would be embarrassed in front of the customers, and as a result his speed, accuracy, and relations with customers would deteriorate. So even though our superior checker is superior in all three categories, she has hurt the total productivity of the operation. Nobody can beat her as far as doing her assigned job is concerned. However, she has failed to live up to good human-relations standards.

In other words, productivity is not only what you do yourself; it is also the influence — good or bad — you have on others. You not only have a job to perform, you have a contribution to make to your fellow employees. It is not a contribution that always comes easily. On occasion you may find it necessary to work effectively with someone you do not like. If you succeed, you have made a worthwhile contribution. If you fail, try to learn something from the experience and wait for another chance, for it is a challenge you should eventually meet successfully. The worker who keeps his or her personal productivity high, and at the same time is sensitive enough to have a beneficial influence on others, is the worker management will probably reward.

Human relations knows no age or experience level. You may be a recent high school or college graduate starting your first job, a middle-aged widow entering the labor market for the first time, a senior citizen taking up a new career, a housewife returning to a job she left years ago, or a long-time career employee just promoted to a management position. Whatever your situation is, human relations will play a vital role in the years that lie ahead.

Once you understand that there is no escape from human relations, you will be in a position to deal with it and to receive the greatest compliment of all: to be recognized, perhaps by a supervisor or a fellow employee, as having the ability to work harmoniously with others. Your knowledge about human relations will have earned you that distinction.

Problem 1

Reality

"It's <u>who</u> you know that counts."

Rod was very pleased with himself when he, along with two equally qualified people, won a job with the Southern Electrical Company. He was assigned to a department that was known for its high productivity and outstanding teamwork. Rod's supervisor told him how lucky he was to win the assignment and then quietly suggested that he make a special effort to get along with everybody.

Rod worked hard and efficiently in his new assignment, but he made a series of human-relations mistakes. For example, he was rude with one co-worker who was slightly late in returning some equipment. Another time he complained that his lunch period was delayed because he had to wait for a fellow employee to return. On still another occasion, he was openly upset when his work load was temporarily increased because a co-worker had to go home sick.

After a few weeks had passed, the supervisor called Rod into his office and had a second, more serious talk with him about the importance of getting along with co-workers. At the end of the interview, Rod asked if his work was satisfactory. The supervisor told him it was substantially above average, but that his human-relations skills could show some improvement.

Some months later Rod heard that the two people who were hired at the same time he was had received promotions. He passed it off by saying, "In this outfit it isn't what you know, but who you know that counts."

Was Rod justified in feeling this way? What might Rod's supervisor have done to help him with his problems? (For a suggested answer, see page 186.)

9

"Who has a split personality?"

CHAPTER 2

HUMAN RELATIONS CAN MAKE OR BREAK YOU

After reading the first chapter, you may have some pressing questions. I answer some of the most frequently asked questions in the pages that follow.

How significant is attitude during the job-interview process?

Critical. Everything on your application form is vital, but your attitude, the way you view work, is equally significant. This, of course, is the purpose of the personal interview. Prospective employers hope to pick up a few signals on how you will work with others and deal with problems. During an interview you communicate with your attitude as well as words.

Will learning more about human relations give me more self-confidence when I meet people for the first time?

Yes. The #1 reward from a study of human relations is greater confidence. More self-confidence will help you take the first step in meeting others, instead of standing on the sidelines thinking about it. You will greet your fellow workers pleasantly, even though they might not return the courtesy. You will feel more at ease about communicating with others. All of this, of course, will greatly help you during the interview process.

Is a quiet person handicapped when it comes to human relations?

Sometimes. People who tend to be quiet need to make a special effort at the beginning. It is difficult to build good relationships with strangers if you back away and refuse to give them a chance to know you.

People who are very quiet or self-sufficient sometimes forget that their silence may be interpreted as aloofness, indifference, or even hostility. To avoid misinterpretation you should learn to communicate frequently and openly with the people you work with. However, it should be encouraging for you to know that many quiet people become highly skilled at human relations later on. The same sensitivity that makes them reserved and reticent also makes them more aware of others' needs.

Can good human relations help one overcome the handicap of youth?

If you can learn to create and maintain good relationships with all people, including those much older than yourself, age need not be a handicap at all. One way to do this is to respect older people's experience and to learn as much as possible from them. The building of such relationships will test your human-relations skills.

Why is it that some sophisticated, capable employees — even managers — seem to ignore good human relations?

It is difficult to understand. Perhaps some assume that they already practice good human relations, or they feel that the subject is too elemental to deal with. Perhaps they permit the pressures of their jobs to push human relations to the bottom of their priority list. They do not realize that when they let this happen they stall their career progress.

Can one become competent in human relations the same way one can become competent as a computer operator, mechanic, or technician?

In a way, yes. It is far more difficult, however, to measure human-relations skills. Nevertheless, people will react in a positive way when you practice good human relations and in a negative way when you don't. So your human-relations skills will be observed, even if they can't be measured precisely. (A list of human-relations competencies is presented on the inside of this book's front and back covers.)

Will paying more attention to human relations give me a brighter future?

Management experts in general agree that those who concentrate on good human relations get the best jobs and eventually rise to the top in most organizations. Those who pay little attention to human relations seem to get lost and are pushed into the least desirable jobs. All organizations are built around people, and when you build healthy relationships with your fellow workers and supervisors, you open doors that would otherwise be closed.

Look at it this way. You have a good education; you have high potential; you have the desire to succeed. All of this is great, but you can't put it to work unless you work well with people — because people, if they want to, can put up roadblocks at every corner. Whether you accept it or not, people will control your job future, and the better the relationships you build with them, the better things will be for you.

Why is human relations more important today than it was thirty or forty years ago?

There are many reasons. Here are five of the most important ones:

1. In previous periods more employees worked alone and therefore did not have to concern themselves with the interpersonal relationships that are necessary to achieve high standards of excellence in a modern business enterprise.

2. Today more workers are employed in service occupations, where the future of the organization depends on how well the customer is served. This makes human relations more important throughout the company.

3. Higher productivity among employees is the key to improved profit and an increase in the standard of living for all people. In order to build superior "work teams," employees need greater competence in human-relations skills.

4. More and more supervisors are being trained in human relations. This can cause a supervisor to set higher human-relations standards and to expect greater human-relations efforts from all employees.

5. The modern work force is composed of a more varied mix of personalities and cultures. Thus, the necessity — and challenge — of building strong human relations with all kinds of people is greater.

Is human relations as important in small organizations as it is in large ones?

Generally speaking, yes. There are some important differences, though, between functioning in large and small organizations. Your progress over the long run may depend more on good human relations in a large company than in a small company. This is true because there is more supervision and more human-relations responsibility in a large company. Some higher positions in these organizations are almost exclusively leadership positions, where human relations is 60 or 70 percent of the total job.

Also, the big companies were the first to introduce human-relations training for supervisors. They are likely to place more importance on it. It follows that because smaller companies may not provide as much training and assistance, you may have to develop human-relations skills on your own.

Will becoming competent in human relations help me become a better supervisor?

Emphatically, yes. Not only will you become a better supervisor, you will become one sooner. The degree to which you develop your human-relations skills now will strongly influence your progress later. Of course, other factors, such as your willingness to work, also play an important role. But the daily application of the techniques you learn through this book will unquestionably have something to do with the pace of your progress. The last chapter in this book deals with this subject.

Are extroverted people automatically good at human relations?

Not necessarily. Human relations is sensitivity to others. Extroverted people are often too concerned with themselves to be good at building relations with others. The skills and principles outlined in this book can be learned and applied by both extroverts and introverts.

Why are some people so obviously awkward at human relations?

That's a tough question because each personality is different. Here are a few possibilities. Some individuals are so self-centered that they think only of themselves and therefore give little consideration to the feelings of others. Some are blinded by ambition to the point where they seriously jeopardize their relationships with others. Still others let their emotions spill over at the wrong time, destroying relationships they have carefully built. It may be hard to admit, but we all make mistakes in building and maintaining relationships with people. None of us will ever be perfect, but we should never stop trying to improve.

Does high academic performance guarantee high performance on the job?

No. An individual can be outstanding academically but very weak in human-relations skills. The work environment is different, people are different, and the objectives in business are different from those in the classroom. It is frequently true that a student who is average in the classroom is outstanding on the job, and vice versa. This can mean that some students who are high achievers academically might have more of an adjustment to make to the world of work than those who get more practical experience along the way.

Is there a relationship between attitude and learning?

Yes. The expression "openness to learning" is used to communicate that when a mind is open (free of blocks, fears, prejudices, hang-ups) it will more readily accept and retain new data and ideas. In short, if a student dreads taking a required course (calculus, chemistry, English, etc.) the chances of success are diminished because the fear constitutes a block to learning. However, through an "attitude adjustment" counseling session with the professor, the block may be partially eliminated. Learning will be easier because the student's attitude is more positive *toward learning*.

Must I change my personality to become better at human relations?

You are what you are, and you cannot become someone else. However, you can change many of your habits, attitudes, and behavior in working with people. You can develop the personality you already have by becoming more effective in human relationships.

What is the connection between attitude and personality?

There is a symbiotic relationship between the two. Personality is generally considered to be the sum total of special physical and mental characteristics that allow you to transmit a unique image to others. The special "blend" that comes through constitutes your personality. When your positive attitude is in charge, the image communicated is at its best.

You may be proud of one or more of your physical characteristics (eyes, posture, smile, etc.). The same may be true of mental traits (ability to learn, patience, determination, etc.). Attitude, however, is the only characteristic that transcends other traits and pulls them together into a more attractive image. The magic of a positive attitude is that it has a way of making your eyes sparkle more brightly, causing your smile to be more engaging, and generally improving your total countenance.

How does this happen?

Your positive attitude can best be viewed as a background "light" that enhances your other characteristics. When you are positive, the traits you desire to feature come to life. They are highlighted. Even your less favorable traits appear more attractive. Your total personality is appreciated and enjoyed more by others.

What is charisma?

Charisma is a special blend of a few physical and mental characteristics that seem to communicate a touch of magic. To most people, President Jack Kennedy had charisma. Many movie stars have it. Most of us do not have recognizable charisma. *But when we have a positive attitude we come close.* And even those individuals who have charisma lose it without a positive attitude.

Do some people needlessly carry around a poor image?

Yes. This is unfortunate because a positive attitude can pull their best traits to the surface and give them a better image of themselves.

Will this book really help me become human-relations competent?

If you give it a try, yes. Your biggest job, of course, will be to apply what you learn in this book on your present job. If you practice a technique long enough, it becomes a habit and you do it automatically. It won't be easy, though, and as I said before, no one is ever human-relations perfect. Your goal is not to become perfect but to become substantially more effective. This will make the difference you need to become successful.

Problem 2

Adjustment

"Don't ask me ... I just work here."

Ann and George were both young, aggressive, and competent. They joined the M. K. Company on the same day and went through the same training program in preparation for identical jobs involving a great deal of close contact with fellow employees.

Although it was not easy, Ann made a good adjustment to her work environment. She was able to do this because of her warm, flexible personality and the application of the human-relations skills she had learned and developed in college. George, on the other hand, made little progress. He appeared rigid and distant to those who worked around him. To a few older and experienced employees he even seemed aloof and hostile. George's supervisor, watching him from a distance, felt he was waiting around expecting others to approach him and be friendly. He seemed to be standing on the sidelines, unable or unwilling to meet people halfway. Perhaps he did not know how to communicate with others.

One day, during lunch, a few weeks after joining the company, George told Ann he was going to look for another job. His reasons were as follows: (1) he felt some co-workers were unfriendly, (2) he resented some of his fellow employees, who seemed excessively critical of him, and (3) he felt his supervisor was trying to push him into a mold of conformity that was simply not his style. Why should he go all out to adjust? After all, building working relationships is a two-way thing. He felt confident he could find another company that would appreciate him more and give him all the freedom he needed to be himself.

What chance do you think George has of finding a job environment that would make him completely happy? Assume you are George's supervisor and willing to spend thirty minutes in a two-way communications session trying to help him and keep him with the firm. What points would you attempt to cover? (For a suggested answer, see page 186.)

CHAPTER 3

"It's hard to stay positive under pressure."

HOLD ON TO YOUR POSITIVE ATTITUDE

Attitude is a common word. You hear it almost every day. Professors use it on campus. Managers discuss it at work. Employment counselors look for it among applicants. No other attribute will have more influence upon your future. A positive attitude can be your most priceless possession.

If you can create and keep a positive attitude toward your job, your company, and life in general, you should not only move up the ladder of success quickly and gracefully, you should also be a happier person. If you are unable to do this, you may find many doors closed to you on the job and your personal life less than exciting.

There are three forms of communication between people. One is the written form—letters, memos, telegrams. The second is the verbal form—face-to-face conversations, telephone conversations, intercom discussions. The third involves the transmission of attitudes.

The first two forms of communication are so important to the profitable operation of an organization that we tend to think they are the only ones. We forget that we also communicate our attitudes through facial expressions, hand gestures, and other more subtle forms of body language. Sometimes people will greet others with a most positive voice, but their body language (negative facial expression) sends a contrasting signal. As the expression claims, sometimes your attitude speaks so loudly others cannot hear what you say.

So every time you report for work, every time you attend a staff meeting, every time you go through a formal appraisal, every time you take a coffee break, and every time you go out socially, be aware that *your attitude is showing.*

Because attitude can play such an important role in your future, let's take a closer look at the meaning of the word itself. *Attitude* is defined by most psychologists as a mental set that causes a person to respond in a characteristic manner to a given stimulus. You have many attitudes, or "mental sets." You have attitudes toward certain makes of automobiles, toward certain social institutions (schools, churches, and the like), toward certain careers, lifestyles, and people.

You also have a wide variety of job attitudes. You build attitudes toward your supervisor and the people you work with, toward the job you do, toward company policies, toward the amount of money you are being paid. In addition to these specific attitudes, you also have a basic, or total, attitude toward your job and toward life itself. Strictly speaking, then, attitude is the *way you look at your whole environment.*

You can look at your job in any way you wish. On the one hand, you can focus your attention on all its negative aspects (odd hours, close supervision, poor location). On the other hand, you can focus your attention on the more positive factors of the job (harmonious work environment, good learning opportunities, good benefits). All jobs have both positive and negative factors. How you choose to perceive yours is an important decision.

Attitude is the way you view and interpret your environment. Some people can push unpleasant things out of sight and dwell largely on positive factors. Others seem to enjoy the unpleasant and dwell on these negative factors.

What you see in life influences your attitude.

If you go around looking for what is wrong with things, wondering why things are not better, and complaining about them, then you will be a negative person in the minds of most people. If you do the opposite — look for what is good and don't focus on unpleasant things — you will be a positive person in the minds of most people.

There is no perfect job or position. One job may have more favorable things about it than another, but all jobs have some unpleasant things. The employee who dwells on the unfavorable factors has a negative attitude. If he (or she) forces himself to look for factors that are favorable, he will slowly become a more positive person.

Therefore, even if you start a new job or assignment with a positive attitude, you must take care that it remains positive. It is possible that you will meet a few people with negative attitudes who will attempt to persuade you to think as they do. These factors could influence you and destroy what otherwise would have been an excellent start.

To be a positive person, you need not think your company is perfect. That would be foolish. You would eventually become disillusioned. On the other hand, unless you feel that the majority of factors are favorable, you will eventually become negative, and you will show it.

The moment you can no longer be positive about your career with your company, your chances for success diminish.

No one can be positive all the time. You will naturally have periods of doubt. These temporary periods will not hurt you seriously. But a day-to-day negative attitude that persists over weeks and months will destroy your future with the organization. If this should happen, and you honestly feel such an attitude is justified, you should resign.

A positive attitude is essential to career success for many reasons.

1. When you are positive you are usually more energetic, motivated, productive, and alert. Thinking about negative things too much has a way of draining your energy. Put another way, a positive attitude opens a gate and lets your inner enthusiasm spill out. A negative attitude, on the other hand, will keep the gate closed.

2. First impressions are important on the job because they often have a lasting effect. Co-workers you meet for the first time appear to have little radar sets tuned in to your attitude. If your attitude is positive, they receive a friendly, warm signal,

and they are attracted to you. If your attitude is negative, they receive an unfriendly signal, and they try to avoid you.

3. A positive employee contributes to the productivity of others. A negative employee does not. Attitudes are caught more than they are taught! Both negative and positive attitudes are transmitted on the job. They are picked up by others. A persistently negative attitude, like the rotten apple in the barrel, can spoil the positive attitudes of others. It is very difficult to maintain a high level of productivity while working next to a person with a negative attitude.

4. Co-workers like you when you are positive. They like to be around you because you are fun. This makes your job more interesting and exciting because you are in the middle of things and not on the outside complaining. When you are negative, people prefer to stay clear of you. A negative person may build good relationships with a few other people (who are perhaps negative themselves), but such a person cannot build good relationships with the majority of employees.

5. The kind of attitude you transmit to management will have a great deal to do with your future success. Management constantly reads your mental attitude, even though you may feel you are successful in covering it up. Supervisors can determine your attitude by how you approach your job, react to directives, handle problems, and work with others. If you are positive, you will be given greater consideration when special assignments and promotion opportunities arise.

If your job involves customer, client, or patient contacts, you should place additional emphasis on everything stated above. Your attitude is significant in all relationships, but it is crucial when you are in a service position.

It is important to realize that a positive attitude is far more than a smile. A smile, of course, is helpful in transmitting an inner positive attitude. However, some people transmit a positive attitude even when they seldom smile. They do this by the positive way they treat others, the way they look at their responsibilities, and the perspective they take when faced with a problem.

Attitude is a highly personal thing. It is very closely tied to your self-concept, to the way you look at yourself. Because of this, attitude is not easy to talk about. People often freeze when the word is mentioned. As a result, management may never talk to you about your attitude. They may never say, for example, "Let's be honest. Your attitude is negative. What are you going to do about it?" *But everyone will know when it is showing.*

How, then, do you make sure you keep your positive attitude when things get tough? How do you keep a good grip on it when you are discouraged? How do you keep it in good repair on a day-to-day basis over the years? Here are a few simple suggestions.

1. *Build a more positive attitude in one environment and you will be more successful in another.* Your positive or negative attitude is not something that you can hang on a hook. It follows you wherever you go. It is reasonable to assume, then, that if you make a greater effort to be a more positive person in your social and personal life, this will automatically spill over and help you on the job. By the same token, if you make a greater effort to develop a more positive attitude at work, this will in turn make a contribution to your social and personal life. One effort will complement the other.

2. *Talk about positive things.* Negative comments are seldom welcomed by fellow workers on the job; nor are they welcomed by those you meet in the social scene. The solution? Be complimentary. Constant gripers and complainers seldom build healthy and exciting relationships with others.

3. *Look for the good things in the people you work with, especially your supervisors.* Nobody is perfect, but almost everybody has a few worthwhile qualities. If you dwell on people's good features it will be easier for you to like them and easier for them to like you. Make no mistake about one thing: people usually know how you react to them even if you don't communicate verbally.

4. *Look for the good things in your organization.* What are the plus factors that make it a good place to work? Do you like the hours, the physical environment, the people, the actual work you are doing? What about opportunities for promotion? Do you have chances for self-improvement? What about your wage and benefit package? Do you have the freedom you seek? No job is perfect. But, if you concentrate on the good things, the negative factors may seem less important. This does not mean that you

should ignore negative elements that should be changed. Far from it! A positive person is not a weak person. A positive person is usually confident, assertive (within limits), and an "agent of change" within an organization. Management is not seeking passive people who meekly conform. They want spirited, positive people who will make constructive and thoughtful improvements.

If you decide to stay with an organization for a long time, you would be wise to concentrate on its good features. This may take a great amount of personal fortitude on your part, but it is the best way to keep your career on an upward track. If you think positively, you will act positively and you will succeed.

5. *Avoid financial problems through planning and discipline.* On campus surveys indicate that students frequently fail academically and "drop out" because of financial problems. It also appears that career employees troubled with "dollar worries" often turn negative and lose the promotions that would provide the extra money that could help them pay off their bills. Unfortunately, few of these individuals realize that their positive attitudes are being sacrificed along with their credit ratings. Instead of seeking and accepting family or professional financial counseling, they permit their insolvency to lead them into attitudinal bankruptcy. When this happens, they pay a double penalty.

6. *Don't permit a fellow worker (or even a supervisor) who has a negative attitude to trap you into his (or her) way of thinking.* You may not be able to change his attitude, but at least you can protect your own positive attitude from becoming negative. The story of Sandy will emphasize this point.

Sandy was a little uneasy about starting her new job. It was a fine opportunity and she knew the standards were very high. Would she have the skills needed? Could she learn fast enough to please her supervisor? Would the older employees like her? Although Sandy's concern was understandable, it was not justified. In addition to being highly qualified for the job, she also had a happy, positive attitude that wouldn't stop. She was seldom depressed.

Everything went very well for Sandy for a while. Her positive attitude was appreciated by all. Slowly, however, her fellow workers and supervisor noticed a change. She became more critical of her colleagues, her job, and the company. Her usual friendly greetings and helpful ideas were gradually replaced by complaints. What had happened? Without realizing it, Sandy was showing the effects of the friendships she had made on the job. Needing acceptance in a strange environment, she had welcomed the attention of a clique of employees who had a negative attitude — a group that management already viewed critically.

Sandy was not able to confine her negative attitude to her job. Soon, again without realizing it, she let her negative attitude spill over into her social life. In fact, it troubled her boyfriend so much that he had it out with her one night. His words were a little rough. "Look, Sandy. When you are happy you are very attractive and fun to be around. But frankly, when you are negative you are a real bore, and I never have a good time with you. I think those so-called friends you hang around with on the job are killing what was once a beautiful personality."

It wasn't a happy evening, but Sandy got the message. She made a vow to recapture and hang on to the positive attitude she had previously enjoyed. Not only was she successful in doing this, but she also converted a few of her previously negative friends to her way of thinking. Her action saved her career.

Holding on to your positive attitude will never be easy. There are many techniques, however, that can help. Some will be discussed later in this book. One that will help you get started, especially when an irritating problem surfaces, is saying the word or expression *serendipity*.

Serendipity was coined by Horace Walpole in 1754 when he put the fairytale *The Three Princes of Serendip* to paper. A modern version by Elizabeth Jamison Hodges was published in 1964. It is a delightful story of three princes who travel from kingdom to kingdom in a lighthearted, compassionate manner. In helping others solve their problems, they are led to the solution of a problem in their own kingdom.

Serendipity lends itself to many interpretations. To some, it is a gift to help them find agreeable things not sought. To everyone it is a "happiness" word. The magic comes into play when we realize a "lighter approach" can often not only solve a problem, but cause something good to happen in our lives.

In short, serendipity is an attitude — a kind of frivolous mental set that can help us view our work environment in a more humorous and forgiving manner. It is an attitude that temporarily moves responsibility aside and encourages one to "rise above" any negative situation. This serendipitous attitude is within the reach of everyone and, when achieved, fortuitous things may happen. For example, when you have a lighthearted, mischievous, festive way of looking at things, others are intrigued and may invite you to share beautiful experiences with them that, in turn, can enhance your life. Serendipity is a state of mind that is symbolized by the clowns on the cover of this book. It is a wonderful attitude to take to a party. There are also times when it can be a lifesaver in the workplace.

You have now completed Part I of this book, which is designed to help you understand yourself and especially the potential of your positive attitude. The next section will introduce you to ways you can use your positive attitude to build and maintain better human relations.

Problem 3

Credit Blues

"Financial solvency helps keep my attitude positive."

Manuel was an art major in college, where his professors constantly praised his work, and he won a number of prizes in campus art shows. Upon graduating, Manuel made many attempts to find a job in commercial art. No luck. After many disappointments, he reluctantly accepted a position with a large retail chain that would only have limited use for his talent in the area of merchandising display.

Manuel decided to make the most of his situation and began his career with a positive attitude. He quickly demonstrated that he had both talent and managerial ability. His future looked bright. He was happy. Some time later, however, his supervisor noticed Manuel's enthusiasm had started to dwindle. He began giving excuses for not getting things done on time. Manuel's art displays were not up to previous standards. His relationships with other workers started to deteriorate.

In a heart-to-heart talk with his sensitive and supportive manager, Manuel revealed that he was having serious financial problems. Through the purchase of a new sports car and other consumer items, Manuel was behind on his credit payments and the high interest rates were keeping him in the hole. Manuel's manager told him he was suffering from a severe case of "plastic blues" and sent him to a company counselor with expertise on financial planning.

Would you agree that financial problems can damage a positive attitude and derail one's career? What suggestions would you make to Manuel to help him stay positive while he digs himself out of his financial hole? (For a suggested answer, see page 187.)

PART **II**

RELATIONSHIPS
WITH
OTHERS

4

"Relationships are <u>that</u> important?"

VERTICAL AND HORIZONTAL WORKING RELATIONSHIPS

Understanding yourself and the power of your positive attitude makes it much easier to meet new people and establish meaningful relationships with them. For example, when you meet a supervisor or co-worker for the first time, a psychological reaction takes place: each person instantaneously interprets the other. It is a feeling that is hard to define. You know something is happening, but you can't put your finger on it. Slowly, as you and the other individual see each other more frequently and get to know each other better, these initial feelings mature into what is called a *relationship*.

A relationship is a *feeling thing* that exists between two people who associate with each other. You can't see, taste, smell or touch a relationship — you can only feel it in a psychological sense. Job relationships are usually different from social relationships. Job relationships exist only because you selected a certain company and were assigned to work with certain people in a specific department. In other words, in your social life you have a choice; on the job you do not. Nevertheless, working relationships are extremely important to you and your future because they will have a strong influence on your personality and personal productivity.

Working relationships of this nature are fascinating to study. For example, one interesting characteristic is that two persons cannot meet regularly on the job or work in the same general areas *without* having a relationship. So the first thing to learn about working relationships is that whether you like it or not, one will exist between you and every employee or supervisor with whom you have regular contact.

- You need not work next to this person.

- You need not speak to her (or him).

- You need not even have a desire to know her.

Yet, a relationship will exist. There appears to be no way to neutralize a relationship under these conditions. The very fact that you might decide to ignore a person does not destroy the relationship; in fact, the opposite may happen. The relationship may become more tense and psychologically powerful. Let us take a specific example.

You notice an employee working in a department next to you. In an attempt to be friendly, you say hello in a very pleasant way to this person the first day on the job, and you receive no reply.

Does this mean the relationship is cut off at this point?

Far from it! You may feel that her failure to reply is a slight to you, and this may naturally disturb you. You may decide not to take the initiative again. Nevertheless, you will remember this person clearly and wonder what will happen in the future.

The person to whom you said hello, on the other hand, has had some kind of reaction to your friendly gesture. She may feel that she treated you in an unfriendly manner (perhaps she was not feeling well that day) and might welcome another opportunity to be more friendly. Or, she may have interpreted your hello as being a little too forward on your part as a new employee and decided to be cool toward you.

You could ignore her. You could avoid verbal contact. You and she could see each other only a few times a week.

Would a relationship exist?

Yes, indeed. Two persons have made contact with each other. They see each other occasionally. They work for the same company. As long as these factors exist, a relationship must exist. Under these conditions you cannot erase a relationship. The attempt on the part of one person to withdraw serves only to make the relationship more emotionally charged; it does not in any manner eliminate it.

You cannot consistently work with or near people or communicate with them frequently without having working relationships with them.

There is another interesting characteristic about these relationships when viewed objectively. They are either strong or weak, warm or cool, healthy or unhealthy, friendly or distant. There appears to be no absolute neutral ground. Every relationship has a very small positive or negative content.

Have you ever heard someone say, "I can take her or leave her"? The phrase usually means that it doesn't make any difference whether the person referred to is around or not. But the very fact that one makes such a comment indicates that it would be better if the person were not around. The relationship still exists, and in this case it is a little cool.

A third characteristic is that each relationship is different. You must build relationships with all kinds of people, regardless of race, religion, age, sex, or personality characteristics. Each relationship will be unique. Each will be built on a different basis. Each will have its own integrity.

As you look around and study your co-workers and your supervisor, you will see that they are all separate personalities. At the same time, your supervisor and co-workers are studying you. Do they all see the same person?

Strange as it may seem, they do not. You do not look the same to different people. You make a different impression on each of them because they interpret you differently.

There is another way of saying this: you do not have a single personality in the eyes of others. Each person interprets you differently — based on his (or her) own unique background, prejudices, likes, dislikes, and so on. Your personality, to that person, is different. The way he interprets your personality *is* your personality to that person.

Why all this emphasis on the way in which people view your personality? How will this help you become more sensitive to human relationships?

Here is your answer. Because everybody sees you differently, you will have to build good relationships with different people differently. And make no mistake here. *Good relationships must be built.* They seldom come about automatically.

You will rarely build a strong, warm, or healthy relationship with two persons in the same way. You will always have to take into consideration the party at the other end of the relationship.

Some people are not going to interpret your personality favorably to start with. You are going to have to be sensitive enough to determine who these people are, and then you must build a good relationship with them on an individual basis. It is not easy to change a cool relationship to a warm one, yet you cannot afford to allow it to remain in an unhealthy state. You should make some effort to build it into a stronger relationship. To do this, you should consider the person at the other end of the relationship and remember that he sees you differently than anyone else.

Now that you have a good picture of just what is meant by a relationship, it is time to talk about the two kinds of relationships.

First we will discuss the *vertical working relationship*. This is the relationship between you and your immediate supervisor. If, as a regular employee, you have two or more supervisors, you will have two or more vertical relationships to maintain. Normally, you will have one immediate supervisor, as illustrated here.

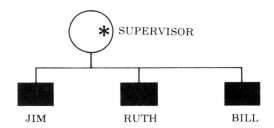

In a small department consisting of one supervisor and three employees, each employee has a different vertical relationship with the same supervisor. This relationship is indicated by the line between each employee and the supervisor. This is often called the *job-relations line*. If the relationship is strong, we indicate this by a heavy line. If it is weak, we indicate this by a light line. Naturally it is almost impossible for the supervisor to create and maintain an equally strong line between himself and all the employees in the department. It is his job to try to do this, and the closer he comes to this ideal the better it is for the department. But supervisors are human beings and are not perfect. Consequently, the job-relations lines are seldom equally strong.

The person working next to you might have a stronger relationship with the supervisor than you have, or she might have a weaker one.

You will notice in the following illustration that arrows have been added to the lines.

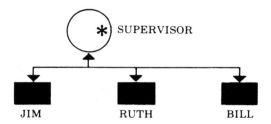

These arrows at the ends of the vertical job-relations lines have real significance. They signify that there should be a free flow of information between the workers and the supervisor. It is extremely difficult for a strong relationship to exist between two persons without two-way communication. The supervisor must feel free to discuss, openly and frankly, certain problems with Ruth, Jim, and Bill. If the supervisor hesitates to talk with Jim about a certain weakness in his job performance, the relationship between the two of them is not what it could be. By the same token, if Jim is hesitant about taking a suggestion or a gripe to the supervisor, the relationship is less than ideal.

The lifeblood of a good relationship is free and open communication. Good relationships are built and maintained by free and frequent verbal communication. People need to talk with each other, exchange ideas, voice complaints, and offer suggestions if they intend to keep a good relationship. The moment that one party refuses to talk things over, the relationship line becomes thin and weak.

The primary responsibility for creating and maintaining a strong vertical relationship rests with the supervisor. This is a responsibility that goes with his position. If the relationship line is in need of repair, it is primarily his responsibility to initiate a discussion that can mend the break.

Although the supervisor has the primary responsibility, you as the employee have the secondary responsibility to keep the relationship line strong and healthy. Some employees make the serious mistake of thinking that the supervisor is wholly responsible for making them happy and productive.

Chapter 7 will show you how to create and maintain a good relationship with your supervisor. It will suffice now to say that you can't expect the supervisor to do all the relationship building. You will have to work hard to keep a good job-relations line between you and your supervisor. Even if you have an exceptionally poor supervisor, you will have to meet him (or her) halfway. Vertical relationships need to be in healthy repair if productivity is to be high in a department. Often the supervisor finds that it requires a great deal of tact and delicacy to maintain vertical relationships. Small wonder that management has seen fit to give him some special training.

The horizontal working relationship is also important to you.

Horizontal working relationships are those that exist between you and fellow workers in the same department—the people you work next to on an hour-to-hour, day-to-day basis. The following diagram illustrates the horizontal relationships between three people in a very small department.

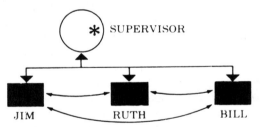

You will note that Jim has a horizontal working relationship with both Ruth and Bill. In this very small department of three employees and one supervisor, Jim has one vertical relationship and two horizontal relationships to keep strong. It is easy to see that in larger departments there would be many more. In fact, the average number of employees in a department is nine.

You (not the supervisor) have the primary responsibility for creating and keeping healthy horizontal relationships. The supervisor—working at a distance in regard to these relationships—has the secondary responsibility. Once in a while she might find it necessary to step in to help restore a good relationship between two employees. But by and large she must leave this up to the employees themselves.

The critical need for building good horizontal working relationships is often ignored by some workers. When they permit this to happen, their doors of opportunity are locked and the keys are thrown away.

It is extremely important to the new employee to build and maintain good horizontal working relationships. In fact, this should be a major part of your total human-relations effort as you start your career. Much of this book is devoted to the principles and techniques that will assist you in this respect. For example, here are two mistakes you should refrain from making:

1. Avoid concentrating on building a good relationship with your supervisor and neglecting good relationships with your fellow workers.

2. Avoid concentrating on building one or two very strong horizontal working relationships and neglecting those with the remaining fellow workers in your department.

Making either mistake will cause immediate disharmony in your department and will put you in human-relations hot water. The supervisor cannot afford to have an extremely strong relationship with you and weak relationships with your fellow workers if he wants high productivity from all. It makes for dissension and immediate cries of favoritism.

From your point of view, then, an overly strong vertical relationship can cause a general weakening of your horizontal working relationships. When you make the mistake of concentrating on one or two horizontal working relationships, the remaining horizontal relationships deteriorate and your vertical relationship with the supervisor is also weakened.

All horizontal working relationships in the same department should be given equal attention and consideration. One should not be strengthened at the expense of others, even though it may be more fun and more satisfying. Balance is important.

When you concentrate on creating good horizontal working relationships with all fellow workers, you almost automatically create a good vertical relationship with your supervisor. It should be recognized, of course, that the success of this principle is assured only if the supervisor is sufficiently sensitive to know what is going on. In the majority of cases, this is a fair assumption. A perceptive supervisor will greatly appreciate any employee who builds a better team spirit in his department by creating and maintaining strong horizontal working relationships.

There are, of course, important relationships other than those indicated in the diagram. Your relationship-building activity should not be confined to a single department. It is a good idea for you to expand your sphere of influence as quickly as possible on your new job. The more good relationships you build, the better.

As important as peripheral relationships are, they are not your primary working relationships. You cannot afford to concentrate on building relationships outside your department by neglecting those on the inside.

The building of a strong vertical relationship with your immediate supervisor and strong horizontal working relationships with your fellow workers is absolutely essential to your personal success. No other human-relations activity should have a higher priority.

Problem 4

Decision

"My supervisor ignores me."

Because of a realignment of personnel, Bernie was transferred (against his wishes) to the traffic department, in which he would have seven horizontal relationships and one vertical relationship to build. Bernie was the junior member. All the other employees, including the supervisor, were much older than he.

After one week in the department, he discovered that his supervisor was difficult to approach and talk to, that he stayed aloof from the workers in the department, and that he often seemed critical. In fact, Bernie could feel a psychological barrier between the supervisor and the rest of the department. Once a week there was a short staff meeting, but most of the employees were silent and somewhat hostile.

How could he build a strong, worthwhile vertical relationship with a man of this nature in an environment that was so structured? Wouldn't he be wiser to concentrate exclusively on horizontal relationships until an opportunity to establish a better relationship with his supervisor presented itself? After giving the matter some serious thought, Bernie decided indeed to concentrate on horizontal relationships and weather it out.

Was this a smart decision on Bernie's part? Would you have gone about it differently? Support your point of view. (For a suggested answer, see page 188.)

CHAPTER 5

"Being productive requires
more than technical skills."

PRODUCTIVITY — A CLOSER LOOK

A manufacturing plant, in order to be competitive with other operations turning out a similar product, must *produce* at the lowest possible cost per single item or unit. A retail store, in order to pay overhead expenses and show a profit, must *produce* sales at a certain level. An airline must *produce* a reliable service that will attract enough customers to keep the seats filled. Even a municipal organization like a fire department must *produce* at a level that will satisfy taxpayers. Every kind of organization must produce, and when production is not sufficient to make a profit or satisfy people, changes are made. These are economic facts of life.

Because productivity is so important, management has devised ways of measuring it. Productivity is easily measured on an assembly line where the worker must perform a specific function, such as connecting a wire or screwing on a nut. This kind of job can be time studied and a standard rate established. If the standard rate is 85 completions in 60 minutes, it means that the average worker can reach and sustain this number over a certain period of time.

Measurable jobs or tasks of this nature are found primarily in the manufacturing and fabricating industries. Other jobs, such as secretarial work, are more difficult to measure because factors such as how much initiative is demonstrated, how people are treated, and how the telephone is answered are difficult to measure.

Productivity, then, can be measured scientifically in some situations, but in countless others it can only be measured by management judgment. Regardless of the kind of job you now hold or the way in which your productivity is measured, understanding what is meant by productivity (from the management point of view) is important to your future.

There are two kinds of productivity.

Individual productivity. Individual productivity is the contribution a single person makes to getting the departmental job done. It is the amount of work one person does in comparison with that of others in the group or section. It may or may not be measurable.

Group productivity. Group productivity is the sum total of all individual contributions, including that of the supervisor. It can be — and often is — measured objectively, that is, reduced to figures and statistics.

Each worker has a current (day-to-day, week-to-week) level of productivity that generally remains constant, although it may fluctuate from time to time. Let us illustrate this through the use of a glass or beaker. Assume that a solid line drawn across the glass is the current level of productivity for a person we will call Jane. Like all employees, Jane also has a potential level of productivity that is greater than her current level.

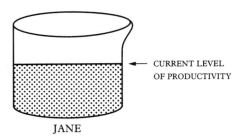

CURRENT LEVEL
OF PRODUCTIVITY

JANE

Seldom, if ever, does a person reach his or her full potential. Jane would be the first to agree with this. So let us draw a dotted line across the glass to indicate Jane's potential level of productivity. We don't know exactly where Jane's potential might be. It is impossible to measure her capacity or potential scientifically because more than her mental ability is involved — and even her mental ability cannot be measured accurately. But for our hypothetical situation, we can say that Jane's potential is substantially above her current level of productivity.

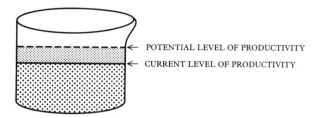

In the preceding diagram then, Jane's current level of productivity is indicated by the solid line, and her potential or possible level of productivity is indicated by the dotted line. The difference between the two is what we will call the *productivity gap*.

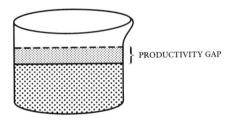

There is always a gap between what one could do and what one actually does. Of course management would like to see Jane close the gap between her current and potential productivity levels as much as possible, but it would be asking too much to expect her to close it completely.

We are concerned, then, not so much with the gap itself as with the size of the gap. If it is small, Jane's supervisor knows she is working close to her capacity. If it is large, the supervisor knows that something is wrong and should be looked into.

Jane's supervisor should, of course, do all she can to keep the distance between Jane's potential and her current performance as small as possible. If the gap becomes too great, she might decide that Jane needs additional training, a special incentive, a change in assignment rotation, or perhaps some form of counseling. The supervisor cannot permit Jane's level of productivity to remain substandard over an extended period of time.

Jane, of course, is not the only worker in the department. In our imaginary situation, let us assume that there are two other employees occupying positions identical to Jane's. These people are called Art and Fred.

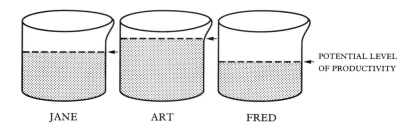

You will note that the potentials of Art and Fred are different from Jane's. It is somewhat disturbing at first to recognize that everyone has his or her potential and that some people have higher potentials than others. However, this is in fact true because everyone differs in mental ability (IQ), ability to endure physical strain (stamina and endurance), ability to perform certain manipulative skills (dexterity), creative level, inner drive, and attitude, as well as in other personality characteristics. All these features together make up an individual's potential.

It is important not to get hung up over the word *potential*. As we are using it, potential simply means the level of productivity a worker might achieve under ideal circumstances if he were pushing himself to his limit. It is seldom, if ever, reached. In using the word *potential*, however, we should remember that some employees are outstanding in some areas, and average or below in others. Few, if any, are outstanding in all areas. Yet, almost everyone has at least one exceptional characteristic.

We need not be concerned about the measurement of potential. (In fact, there is no scientific way to measure it.) All that we need be concerned about is that individual differences exist and that, except under extremely rare conditions, there is always a gap between one's potential and present level of productivity.

In the following diagram, Art has been arbitrarily given a potential above Jane's and Fred's. Fred, on the other hand, has been given a potential below Jane's and Art's.

Now, to complete our diagram, let us assign a current productivity level to each of the three workers.

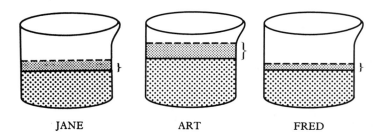

JANE   ART   FRED

You will note that even though Art has a higher potential than Jane, there is not a substantial difference between their current levels of performance. This is a compliment to Jane and perhaps indicates that she is more highly motivated to succeed and consequently performs closer to her potential.

Fred also deserves a compliment because the gap between his current level of productivity and his potential is smaller than that for either Jane or Art. Fred is doing an excellent job in living up to his potential. Perhaps with more education and training, Fred will be able to raise his potential gradually and, in turn, increase his productivity.

Just as each individual has a current and potential level of productivity, so does each branch, division, or department of an organization. This we call *group productivity*.

The next diagram illustrates this important concept. The beaker represents the productivity level and potential of the department as a whole.

CURRENT LEVEL
OF GROUP
PRODUCTIVITY

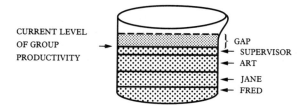

You will observe that the productivity levels of Fred, Jane, and Art (from the previous illustration) have been added to that of the supervisor. As you can see, the supervisor does not contribute as much in productivity (actually getting the work out) as do the individual employees. Why not?

The answer is simple. The primary responsibility of the supervisor is to help each worker achieve his or her maximum productivity. The supervisor's secondary responsibility (as a working supervisor) is to get a certain amount of work done himself. He (or she) cannot be expected to take care of his many supervisory responsibilities and also do as much work as one of the employees in his department. His concern is the *total department productivity*, for this is how he is measured by management.

You will also notice that there is a gap in the department beaker just as there was in the others. This is a *departmental gap*. Just as an individual has a certain potential for productivity, so does a department.

A crew working for a telephone company might have the potential for installing 120 telephones in a certain period of time, and yet actually install only 80. A retail store might have the potential for selling $5,000 worth of merchandise on a day when everything is ideal, and yet on most days sell only $2,000 worth. A claims department for an insurance company might have the potential for processing 50 claims per day, and yet never reach this goal. Just as there is a gap with individuals, there is one with departments and organizations.

It is the responsibility of the supervisor to close the gap between what his department is currently doing and what it might do in the future. There are two ways a supervisor can do this. One is by working harder himself, putting in more hours and making better use of his time. Because he is only one person, there is a limit to what he can do by himself to reduce the size of the gap.

The second — and by far the more effective way to reduce the gap — is to reduce the gaps between the levels of each employee. The productivity of the department is the sum total of the productivity of all members of the department, including the supervisor. The supervisor is interested in each worker's productivity because of what each can contribute to the total.

What should this basic principle mean to you?

Simply this: all employees in a department are interdependent as far as departmental productivity is concerned. If you raise your personal productivity, but at the same time take away some of the productivity of others in the department (because of poor human relations), you have not necessarily added to the total.

Sound strange?

To demonstrate this vital fundamental, let us take Art as an example. The following diagram tells us that Art has a high potential and a good level of productivity. In fact, he is currently producing more than either Jane or Fred.

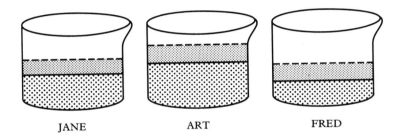

JANE   ART   FRED

But let us assume for a moment that Art begins to ignore Jane and Fred. He is no longer interested in helping them. He refuses to pitch in and do some of their work when they are absent. He starts to rub them the wrong way. His superior attitude causes resentment. Instead of natural, healthy competition, the situation becomes personal and vindictive.

What could happen then?

The productivity of Jane and Fred could drop because of the lack of harmony in the department.

Now let us see what might happen if Art does just the opposite. Let us assume that he becomes more sensitive about human relations. Instead of antagonizing Jane and Fred, he starts working with them. He takes up some of the slack when they are absent. He compliments them on certain skills. He earns their respect instead of their animosity. What happens? Harmony replaces disharmony.

Instead of a wider gap between the current and the potential productivity levels of Jane and Fred, there is a smaller gap. Both

Jane and Fred produce more because Art has strengthened his horizontal relationships with them.

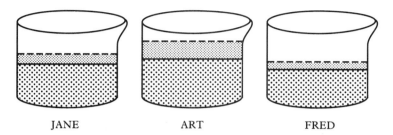

JANE   ART   FRED

This interdependence between workers in a department cannot be ignored. *Group* productivity is the key more than *individual* productivity.

It should be pointed out, however, that sometimes a single individual can raise his or her productivity above that of co-workers; and even though relationships are not ideal, the co-workers will strive to increase their personal productivity so that the other worker will not show them up. The reaction of employees in each situation is different.

Let's review what we have discussed in this chapter.

You have learned that there is always a gap between an individual's current level of productivity and his or her potential. If the employee consistently has a small gap, he is trying hard to contribute and should be complimented by his supervisor for working close to his potential.

There is a departmental gap that represents the difference between what a department can do and what it is actually doing. If the departmental gap is small, the supervisor is doing a good job and should be complimented by her or his superiors.

The human-relations behavior of one worker impacts upon the productivity gap of co-workers as well as that of the department.

Problem 5

Message

"Now you tell me..."

Jeff was one of several employees in a small department where productivity depended upon the close cooperation of everyone involved. He had a high potential and lived up to it, producing more than anyone else in the department.

But Jeff happened to like to work alone. He seldom volunteered to help his fellow workers. Many of the people who worked with him felt he had a superior attitude, and they resented it. As a result, the department was split between Jeff and the others.

Jeff's supervisor gave a lot of thought to the problem and looked at it this way: Although Jeff was producing at the highest level in the department, the total productivity of the department had not gone up since he joined the group. Instead it had gone down slightly. Could it be that Jeff had done more damage (through poor human relations) than good (by his high personal productivity)? The supervisor came to the conclusion that Jeff was an outstanding employee when viewed alone, but a very poor one when viewed as a member of a group.

A few weeks later, the supervisor was promoted to a more responsible position, and management had to come up with a replacement. They decided to promote someone from outside the department. When Jeff discovered that he was not chosen, he demanded an explanation. He was told that he was the highest producer in the department, but his human-relations skills were not up to standard. Management felt the other workers in the department would not respect him as their supervisor.

Do you agree with management's decision to pass over Jeff, even though Jeff was the best producer? Give reasons why you agree or disagree. How responsible do you feel the supervisor was for Jeff's being passed over? (For a suggested answer, see page 188.)

CHAPTER **6**

"High productivity and good
relationships, too?"

THE WINNING COMBINATION

There is a danger of misinterpretation in discussing human relations and productivity. You might have deduced from the last few chapters that building strong and healthy vertical and horizontal working relationships automatically results in greater departmental productivity. This is not necessarily so.

An employee can be happy, satisfied, and content with his (or her) job and yet not carry his fair share of the work load. A group of employees in a department can be getting along beautifully with each other, and yet the productivity of the department might be far below average.

Happy employees are usually — but not always — high producers.

The goal of good human relations is not just happy employees, but *happy employees that produce more.* The goal is greater productivity and ultimately greater profit. It is theoretically possible that a business organization could devote so much time and money to making employees happy and comfortable that the company could go broke and out of business. Management is therefore not interested in making people happy just because happy people are nice to have around or because happy people stick with their jobs longer. Management is interested in making their employees happy because happy employees, under the right leadership, can be motivated to greater productivity.

This should not be interpreted as meaning that employers are

50

sensitive to their employees' needs only because they are interested in increasing productivity. This is not true. Nevertheless, management (and their employees) must fully accept the economic truth that survival under free competition requires a continual improvement in personal and group productivity.

The employee who is fun to be around but never gets down to doing his share of the work is a burden on his fellow workers. He is a parasite on the productivity of others. He may be pleasant to have around, but he is far too expensive for management to keep.

- The work itself must be done.

- Labor costs must be controlled.

- Customers must be well served.

Greater productivity must be the goal of American business organizations if they are to survive and compete with other world markets where labor costs are much lower. The development and use of more and more highly technical equipment will take us a long way, but human productivity must do the rest.

It is only natural, then, that management should seek outstanding people for jobs that are increasingly sophisticated. It is only natural that they should try to find, hire, and train people who have already developed their human-relations skills to a high level.

What are the human factors management seeks?

The most important one is the *right combination of personal productivity and human relations*. The best way to explain this fundamental is to present another hypothetical situation.

This time we will assume that there is a small department composed of three employees who have identical assignments and similar work loads. We will further assume that Alice and Richard have been employed in their positions for over a year. Hazel, on the other hand, joined the organization yesterday as a replacement for an employee who resigned. She has a very high potential, substantially above that of the other two people.

Alice and Richard have been taking it very easy in the department, and there is a sizable gap between their current level of productivity and their potential. In other words, they have not been motivated to do the kind of job they can do. Hazel, however, is very ambitious. She wants to build a reputation for herself and, if possible, move on quickly to a supervisory position where she will have more responsibility and remuneration. In order to gain the attention of management, Hazel decides to increase her personal level of productivity to the point where it will surpass both Alice's and Richard's. She has decided she can do this in either of two ways:

1. She could go all out and pass Alice and Richard in a hurry. But in using this approach she would risk building poor horizontal working relationships with her fellow workers.

2. She could pass Alice and Richard in personal productivity on a somewhat slower and less obvious schedule. This way she could concentrate on building good horizontal relationships with her fellow workers and create a harmonious environment that would increase their productivity along with her own.

What might happen if Hazel decided to follow the first approach and ignore building good horizontal relationships?

It is possible, of course, that Alice and Richard might become motivated. Perhaps in order to make their positions more secure, they might compete with Hazel, and as a result the productivity of the entire department might increase.

It is just as likely, however, that the outcome will be not as positive. Alice and Richard might resent Hazel and, rather than work with her, might in subtle ways work against her. For example, because they are more experienced, they might let her make some mistakes that they could prevent if they wanted to. They could do many little things that would make her uncomfortable and her work more difficult. As a result, Hazel might become critical of Alice and Richard, and the relationships among the three could deteriorate to a point where the productivity of all three would drop. This would be especially serious if customers were involved.

This might not happen, of course — but it could. And if it did, Hazel would certainly not have helped her future with the company. It is not a safe approach for her to take. She could be asking for trouble.

Now what might happen if Hazel took the opposite approach — if she passed Alice and Richard in personal productivity but at the same time worked hard to build good, strong working relationships with them?

It is likely that Hazel would make her job easier. She would be valued more by the supervisor. She would earn the support of both Alice and Richard. She would contribute more to productivity. Instead of falling into a human-relations trap, she would demonstrate to management that she had insight and sensitivity.

Of course it would be easy to tell Hazel that building good working relationships with Alice and Richard is the best route to take. But how should she go about doing it? Here are four suggestions:

1. Hazel could build better horizontal relationships with Alice and Richard if she would sacrifice a little of her personal productivity to help increase theirs. She could accomplish this by looking for opportunities to help Alice and Richard when their work load is heavy or when they do not feel well. She could also pitch in when one of them is absent.

2. As Hazel brings her personal productivity above that of Alice and Richard, she should be careful not to become critical of them because their performance levels are now lower than hers. She should not expect constant praise from her supervisor just because she is, at this point in her career, carrying a larger share of the work load.

3. Hazel should be careful not to isolate herself too much from Alice and Richard. Even if she is occasionally rejected by them, she must continue to be pleasant until good relationships are built. She must be sincerely interested in both Alice and Richard as individuals in order to win their respect. A superior attitude on her part will defeat any effort she makes to build sound relationships.

4. Above all, Hazel should stand on her own two feet and work out her own problems without complaining or running to the supervisor for help. She can only achieve the support of Alice and Richard by demonstrating to them that she knows what she is doing and can fight her own battles.

Hazel will go a long way in communicating to management that she has one of the human-relations plus factors they seek if she keeps the following principle in mind: *An increase in personal productivity should be accompanied by increased attention to horizontal relationships.*

Last week Hazel was invited to have a long talk with the human resource director of her company. During the conversation she asked the director what kind of a person management was really seeking. The director said that management usually sought four plus factors in the employees they hoped to promote into management. Hazel made a big effort to remember all four, and this is the way she would probably put it if you asked her about them now.

1. *The person management is looking for is someone who strives to work close to her (or his) personal potential regardless of the level at which her fellow workers are performing.* She is always trying to close her personal productivity gap, even if others are content to do only what they have to in order to keep their jobs. She is self-motivating. She takes a professional approach to her job and gains real satisfaction when she does it well.

2. *She is never completely satisfied with her personal potential.* She believes that she can always improve it a little. She truly believes in lifelong learning. She takes advantage of any training that the company will provide. She continues to read and study on her own. She is always learning more and more about the job ahead of her. She may even continue her formal education by attending classes at a nearby adult education center, junior college, or university. Although she is realistic about her potential, she does not go along with the idea that a person is born with a certain potential that cannot be changed. She will continue to learn and to prepare for new opportunities.

3. *She believes human relations is important.* She puts people and the development of good human-relations skills ahead of machines, statistics, procedures, and credentials. She accepts responsibility for building strong relationships as an interesting and inevitable challenge. She is highly productive, and at the same time she protects her relationships with people. She does this with a sense of humor and personal understanding. She is proud of the fact that she is a good person to work next to. She endeavors to keep all relations on a sincere level. She does all of this because she knows that she contributes to the productivity

of her department in two ways: one, through her own personal work effort; and two, through the relationships she builds with her fellow employees. She refuses to sacrifice one for the other, and she constantly tries to keep them in proper balance.

4. *She makes a point of being loyal to her company or organization.* This does not mean that she automatically accepts all of the policies and practices that filter down from the top. Far from it. She accepts the responsibility of making changes, but she remains loyal to her company while fighting to bring such changes about. She feels that her company deserves her best effort. She refuses to let human-relations problems, the negative attitudes of others, or personal disappointments slow her down.

Hazel asked the director a second question: "How many employees will I find in this company that have all of the four plus factors?"

He replied: "It is impossible to say. There are many who are good at one or two, some who are good at three, but only a few who are good at all four. At any rate, those who demonstrate all four do not remain line employees for long, unless by choice, because they are desperately needed for supervisory positions."

Hazel then posed her last question: "How does management single out those who have the plus factors they seek?"

"It's easy," replied the director. "You only have to be slightly taller than others to stand out in the crowd. It's the same with the plus factors. You don't have to be miles ahead of others for management to recognize you; a little is all it takes."

Productivity ultimately involves the quality of service provided to customers.

When new employees enter the work force, their main interest is usually career advancement. This is encouraged because a strong focus on personal goals is motivating and has many other beneficial aspects to both employee and employer. But if self-interest goes too far, it can detract from the responsibility to fulfill job duties. A primary responsibility, often neglected by otherwise excellent employees, is developing an effective *service attitude*.

A service attitude is a desire to satisfy customers to the point that they will continue to use the firm's services and bring in new clients, as well. Every employee should take time to identify who their customers are and then serve them in every way possible with a positive attitude. This strategy will create a win-win situation for the client and the company. *Career advancement will be facilitated for the employee.*

It is easy to identify clients when you are on the front line providing *direct* customer service. A waitress, bank teller, doctor, or salesperson receives daily reminders. But what about a machinist, software engineer, or hospital dietician? Although these individuals may not service clients *directly*, they all have service-attitude responsibilities.

The machinest's client may be a manufacturer who assembles the parts he builds into kitchen appliances. Thus, the service attitude of the machinest involves building durable parts, meeting production schedules, and conforming to specifications. The machinest may never *see* the client, but he is building a quality product that serves him indirectly. The hospital dietitian serves those who will eat the food prepared by others. The software engineer's clients are those who will eventually utilize the computer programs. All can benefit from a positive *service attitude*

> Let's look at Sid and Lisette. Both design computer software for financial institutions. Both are highly professional and career minded. The primary difference between them is their service attitudes.
>
> Sid works closely with his own boss and the manager of the financial organization being served to get the specifics of each job before designing his software package. He does not take time to consult with the ultimate users — tellers and other front-line employees. Even so, Sid receives many compliments from his boss because he is always on or ahead of schedule.
>
> Lisette, on the other hand, takes the time to get specifics directly from users (branch managers, new account officers, tellers), who are the ultimate clients. This takes more time, so Lisette does not always receive immediate reinforcement from her boss. Most of the time her compliments show up later, but they are more meaningful because they demonstrate a superior service attitude.
>
> Each individual must identify her or his clients and design a strategy that will best serve them, whether compliments are received or not.

Problem 6

Insight

"Okay, next time I'll cool it."

Ted had been with the Kramer Corporation for more than nine months. From his first day, he had been determined to set a pace that would earn him a promotion. It took him a little while to catch on to the job, but within four months he was up to the average of others in productivity. After a few more months, he was the top producer in the department. In the meantime, the others maintained a steady, but slower pace.

Ted felt good about his ability to pass others in the department, but he was disturbed because he had received so little recognition for the achievement. In fact, the harder he worked, the more difficult it was to get along with the others. Even the supervisor had failed to give Ted as much encouragement as he felt he deserved.

After a few weeks of being the top producer, Ted became more critical of the others. He started to give out a few tips on how they might improve their efficiency, and he began to sound off more in staff meetings.

One day the whole situation reached a boiling point. Ted was strongly counseled by his supervisor to be more patient and understanding with his fellow workers. "Look, Ted," said his supervisor. "You've got it all going for you, but you will never win a promotion if you blow your cool with your fellow employees. You have a very high potential and your productivity is great, but you can't expect others to always equal your pace. I don't want you to destroy now the very relationships you might have to rebuild later should you take my place."

Was Ted's exasperation justified? Or did his supervisor have a good point? (For a suggested answer, see page 189.)

CHAPTER 7

"I understand my supervisor perfectly."

YOUR MOST IMPORTANT WORKING RELATIONSHIP

The most important working relationship you must deal with is the one between you and your immediate supervisor. This single relationship can speed up your personal progress or slow it down to a discouraging crawl. It can make going to work a joy or a drag. It can prepare you for greater responsibilities or it can frustrate your desire to learn. And there is just no way to avoid the human-relations fact that, good or bad, you must learn to cope with your boss.

What kind of person will you draw as a supervisor?

It is impossible to predict. However, he (or she) will be basically the same person he used to be when he held a job similar to yours, except that now he has much more responsibility. He may or may not have been given some special training to help him become a good supervisor. He may be easy to get along with or he may be very difficult. He may be sensitive to your needs or he may be insensitive. He may be feeling his way along and making many mistakes, or he may be highly experienced and a real pro at his job.

Three things are certain about your supervisor, however: (1) he probably has a strong personality that gave him the confidence to become a supervisor in the first place, (2) the responsibilities of being a supervisor probably weigh heavily on his shoulders, and (3) he has work authority over you.

What is a supervisor?

He or she is a *teacher*. He will not only teach you the routine of your new job, but he will also have a great influence on your attitude toward your job and the company. He has a reservoir of knowledge, skills, and techniques that you need to learn. You will be most fortunate if he is a good teacher. If he is not, you will have to learn from observation.

He is a *counselor*. His job is to see that you live up to your potential. He may need to correct errors you are making. He may need to give you tips on improving yourself as an employee. He may feel the need to have a heart-to-heart talk with you at times.

He is a *leader*. More than anything else, your supervisor must provide the leadership your department requires. He must provide motivation for all employees. He must earn your respect — not by being soft and easy, but by being a strong leader who will help you build a long-range career.

It would be a mistake to attempt to type supervisors. They cannot be clearly classified into different groups. Each supervisor has a unique personality. Each has his or her own style.

Do you recall your early school days, when you discovered the differences between teachers? you may have had one who expected a great deal more from you than the others. You may not have liked this person at the time, but years later you came to realize how much this one teacher had taught you. The same can be true with supervisors.

If you are ambitious, you don't want an easygoing supervisor who does not care and, as a result, hinders instead of helps your progress. You will be better off with a more concerned, more demanding supervisor who will help you reach your potential. With an easy supervisor, you might develop some poor working habits and eventually become unhappy with yourself. With a strong supervisor, one who will take time to train you, you will become a better worker and improve your future. But no matter what kind of boss you encounter, it is up to you to learn to understand him and work efficiently under his kind of leadership.

You should do some of the adjusting.

You should provide some of the understanding.

You should help build the relationship that must exist between the two of you.

Each individual supervisor creates his own special climate,

or atmosphere, under which you must operate. The following analysis of three kinds of climates may give you some indication of the adjustments you might have to make in the future.

The Structured Climate

Some supervisors are more strict than others. They operate a tight department by keeping close, and sometimes restrictive, controls. They frequently expect employees to be precisely on time, orderly, and highly efficient. They permit foolishness only when a special occasion calls for it. Ninety-eight percent of the time they stick strictly to business.

The supervisor who creates this kind of atmosphere often appears cold, distant, and unfeeling to the new employee. He (or she) seems unreachable. As a result, the new employee may begin to fear him.

Some jobs force supervisors to be autocratic. Some kinds of work require a very high level of safety standards and efficiency. For example, a producer of a television program might have to be autocratic in order to maintain the level of split-second efficiency required. Work of a highly technical nature, in which certain precision standards must be met, will call for a different climate than work in a service field.

Although the supervisor who establishes this kind of atmosphere may appear cold and unapproachable, the opposite is often true. He is probably more interested in you and more willing to help than you suspect.

The Permissive Climate

The direct opposite of the structured climate is the permissive atmosphere. Some supervisors have a free-and-easy leadership style. There is no apparent intervention and there are few controls or restrictions.

The permissive climate can be the most dangerous of all, especially for the inexperienced employee because his (or her) need for self-discipline is so great. If he does not feel the presence of a leader, he may not make good use of his time. He may find it difficult to motivate himself. If things are too easygoing, he may relax too much and become too friendly with fellow workers. All of this can create bad habits that will ultimately lead to mutual dissatisfaction. Instead of being an ideal situation, then, the permissive climate becomes a trap that can destroy the desire to succeed and eventually cause great unhappiness.

Whether we like to accept it or not, a structured climate often gives us more job security and forces us to live closer to our potential. Beware of a climate that is too relaxed unless you are a self-starter and can discipline yourself. You might discover that too much freedom is your downfall.

The Democratic Climate

The goal of most supervisors in modern organizations is to create a democratic climate. This atmosphere is the most difficult of all to establish. In fact, purely democratic action is often a goal rather than a reality.

A democratic climate is one in which the employees want to do what the supervisor wants done. The supervisor becomes one of the group and still retains his (or her) leadership role. He permits the employees to have a great deal to say about the operation of the department. Everyone becomes involved because each person works from inside the group rather than from outside. The supervisor is the leader and a member of the group at the same time. As a result, a team feeling is created. Many isolated cases of research indicate that most people experience greater personal satisfaction and respond with greater productivity if the supervisor can create and maintain a democratic atmosphere.

If this is true, why can't more supervisors achieve this kind of climate? There are many reasons.

In the first place, it is the most difficult climate to create, and once created, the most difficult to maintain. It requires a real expert, an individual with great skill and sensitivity; *one should not expect to find a great number of supervisors with this ability.*

In the second place, not all workers respond to this climate, ideal as it may seem. You may like it best, but others in your department may like a more autocratic approach. This is especially true when there are young workers in a department where many more experienced and older employees work. You will often hear employees say: "I wish he would quit fooling around and tell us what to do" or "I wish she would tighten up things around here — those people are getting away with murder" or "He is too easy. I can't enjoy working for someone who doesn't set things down clearly and specifically from the beginning."

In the third place, the supervisor who aspires to build a true democratic climate always finds himself (or herself) somewhere between the structured and the permissive. He may approach the ideal situation for a while, only to find that a few employees are taking advantage of him. When this happens it is necessary to tighten up again and become more structured.

All supervisors must create and maintain what some people refer to as a *discipline line*. This is an imaginary line or point beyond which the employee senses she or he should not pass lest some form of disapproval and possible disciplinary action take place. It is important to keep a consistent discipline line. Some supervisors claim that keeping a firm, but comfortable one is a tightrope they walk each day on the job.

You may hear your supervisor or a college professor discuss Theory X and Theory Y. *Theory X* (representing a more structured climate) supports management by control. It states that the worker should be directed and controlled in order to achieve high productivity. A basic assumption is that most employees are not self-motivated. Leaders with a Theory X orientation often reach consistently high productivity levels in their departments. They also have the reputation of doing an excellent job in training their employees.

Theory Y (representing a more democratic/permissive climate) encourages participative management. It states that the worker will achieve greater productivity if he (or she) can set his own goals and direct his own efforts through involvement. The theory assumes that under the proper working climate workers will motivate themselves. A discipline line is maintained at a lower level. Theory Y leaders who are sufficiently skillful to achieve high productivity demonstrate a high level of leadership talent that often attracts the attention of upper management.

Theory Z is more a corporate than an individual leadership style.* A Theory Z company demonstrates unusual responsibility toward its employees and asks for a high degree of loyalty and performance in return. Theory Z firms go to great pains to avoid layoffs and to involve their employees in establishing departmental productivity goals. Under this kind of management, each organization (Hewlett-Packard, IBM, and Procter & Gamble are generally held up as examples) develops a distinctive corporate culture with traditions and ideals that persist over time.

Every supervisor creates his or her own individual climate. Some supervisors come up with a workable blend of the structured and democratic. Others come up with a blend of the permissive and democratic. We call this their *management, or leadership, style.*

Whether we personally like a supervisor or his style is not as important as whether we can learn to be productive in the climate he creates. The new worker should not be too quick to judge, however, because it is often true that what appears to be a difficult climate at the beginning might turn out to be a comfortable and beneficial one later on. So whatever the *style* of the supervisor you draw, it will be your responsibility to build the best possible relationship with him or her. Your career progress may depend upon it. To help you meet this challenge, here are ten tips that should assist you.

1. *Avoid transferring to your supervisor the negative attitudes you may have developed toward other authority figures in your life.* Some people who have had problems with other supervisors, parents, teachers, and similar authority figures make the mistake of transferring their feelings of hostility to their new supervisor. This is unfair. Wipe away any previous negative feelings you may have, and give your new (or present) boss an opportunity to build a healthy relationship with you. If you give her (or him) a fair chance, she will almost always earn your respect instead of your hostility.

2. *Expect some rough days under her supervision.* Everyone, including supervisors, is entitled to a few bad days. Your boss is only human. If she should boil over on a given day, don't let it

---

*William Ouchi, *Theory Z: How American Business Can Meet the Japanese Challenge* (Reading, Mass.: Addison-Wesley, 1981.)

throw you. If she seems to be picking on you for a while, give her time to get over it. More important than anything else, try not to take personally anything she does that you don't like. There may be times when you do not understand you boss's behavior, but if you can float along with it, chances are good that it won't last long.

3. *Refuse to nurse a small gripe into a major issue.* A small gripe, when nurtured, can get blown out of proportion and can lead to a confrontation with your supervisor that will hurt your relationship. If you have a legitimate gripe, try to talk it over with her quickly so that you can get it out of your system before it builds up. Remember, she won't know you have a complaint unless you tell her.

4. *Select the right time to approach your supervisor.* Whether you have a complaint or a positive suggestion to make, try to approach your supervisor at the right time. She may be too busy or under too much pressure on a given day to talk to you. If so, wait it out. When the pressure is off, chances are good that she will give you a fair opportunity. However, if you do try to talk to her at a bad time—and are turned off—wait until another day and try again. If it is important to you, she will no doubt want to talk to you about it. Give her another chance.

5. *Never go above your supervisor's head without talking to her first.* The easiest and quickest way to destroy your relationship with your supervisor is to go over her head on a problem that involves her or her department. Always talk to your supervisor first. If you are not satisfied with the results, you can then take other action. At least this way your supervisor will know that you consulted her first.

6. Try not to let your supervisor intimidate you. Keep in mind that your boss may not be a professional. He or she could be guilty of sexual harassment, playing favorites, and other forms of nonprofessional behavior. Such behavior could cause you to fear your boss. Fear is a strong emotion. If you become so fearful of your boss that you cannot approach her, you should talk to someone in human resources, consider a possible transfer, or, if necessary, resign. You will never be happy working for a

person you fear, and a supervisor will seldom respect you if you are afraid of her.

7. *It can be a human-relations mistake to make a buddy of your supervisor.* Your relationship with your supervisor is a business relationship. Keep it that way. The distance between you and your boss may often appear to be a fine line, but she is still your boss. If you get too personal, it will almost always turn out badly.

8. *In case you make a mistake, clear the air quickly.* If you make a serious goof and injure your relationship with your boss, why not clean the slate with an open discussion? It is a good idea to leave work every day with a pleasant feeling toward your job and your supervisor. If you have had trouble with her on a given day and truly believe that it is partly your fault, the mature thing to do is to accept your share of the blame. You will feel better and so will your supervisor.

9. *Remember that not all supervisors enjoy their roles.* A surprising number of supervisors would really prefer to be workers, but they have accepted their promotions because management has pressed them into it, because they feel they can contribute more as supervisors, or because they can make more money to help their families. As an employee, you should view this as a possibility. It will give you more insight into the role itself and perhaps help you tolerate your supervisor more. Try to remember that being a good supervisor is difficult. Sometimes those who try the hardest to win the respect of their workers never fully succeed because of personality traits they cannot change.

10. *When possible, convert your supervisor into a mentor.* A mentor is a person in a key position who takes a personal interest in your career and acts as an adviser. Your present supervisor may be on her way up in your organization. If you build the right relationship with her, she might counsel and guide you over a period of time, even though she may no longer be your supervisor. You might even ride her coattails to the top.

It should be remembered, however, that ethical behavior on the part of both you and your supervisor is essential if the relationship is to be strong and lasting. To maintain your side of the bargain, the following tips are presented.

- Maintain open and honest communication. Tell the whole story regarding any problems that develop. The moment deception appears, the relationship is permanently injured.

- Do not discuss your supervisor in a negative way with coworkers. It communicates an absence of loyalty and is considered by many to be unethical. You need not approve of everything your supervisor does, but it is best to keep it to yourself.

- Refuse to be influenced by either your supervisor or coworkers to perform unethical acts. A good way to take your stand on any questionable situation is to ask openly: "Is this ethical?"

In summary, building and maintaining a strong, warm, productive relationship with your boss is a real human-relations challenge. It isn't always easy. Yet it is an essential step in your progress. You may be used to one supervisor only to discover that you have been transferred to another department and have to start from scratch. Every relationship will be a unique challenge. Make the most of every experience.

Problem 7

Choice

"I'm a Theory Y person myself."

Carol is a career employee with a large organization. For the last sixty days she has been training for a new position and assignment. She has just received word to report to the training department to discuss her new role in the company.

The director gives her a choice of assignments. She tells Carol that two departments have requested her services. The departments are identical in their operations. The only difference is between the supervisors of the two departments and the type of climate each creates. Carol is given the opportunity to observe both supervisors in action.

One department has a rather demanding supervisor who has a leadership style that leans in the direction of Theory X. He believes in rather rigid performance standards and controls. He is an old-timer and has been in charge of his department for many years. He expects and gets high productivity and loyalty from all his employees. Everyone admits that he has trained more people who are now in top management positions than anyone in the company.

The other department is run by an up-and-coming younger supervisor who adheres to Theory Y. She tries to get everyone in the department to participate in decisions and get involved. She prides herself on her democratic leadership style and feels she has been very successful. People appear very happy working for her. The personnel turnover is less in this department than in the other. Productivity is slightly higher.

Which department would you select? On what basis? (For a suggested answer, see page 189.)

CHAPTER 8

UNDERSTANDING THE NATURE OF RELATIONSHIPS

The purpose of this chapter is to look more deeply into the nature of working relationships. To do this we will explore six different characteristics that are often involved. These characteristics can have a considerable influence on the quality or tone of the relationship. In a sense, they constitute the ingredients, or components, that make up the relationship itself. From another point of view, they represent six human-relations competencies you may wish to possess.

Perhaps you will understand the idea of a relationship better if you visualize it as an invisible tunnel between two fellow employees. Disregard the personalities involved and concentrate on the relationship itself. The following illustrations may help you do this.

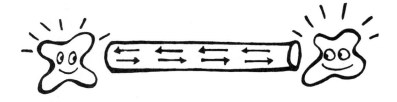

The two-way arrows between the amoebas remind us that verbal communication is the lifeblood of the relationship. Good input and good reception are necessary at both ends. The following illustration adds to the relationship those factors we will deal with in this chapter.

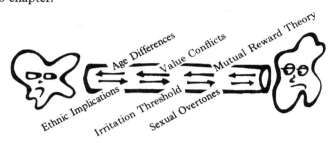

Of course, not all of the above elements are likely to be present in any single relationship. Some relationships may have only one or two. Others may have four or five. An investigation into each of the above, however, will give you additional insight into the nature of all working relationships.

Mutual Reward Theory

With proper care, you can create working relationships that will turn out to be mutually rewarding. The mutual reward theory (MRT) states that a relationship between two people is enhanced when there is a satisfactory balance of rewards between them. In a good MRT relationship, both parties come out ahead. In fact, if a working relationship is to remain healthy over a long time, it must contribute something of value to both persons. When one individual suddenly discovers that she (or he) has been contributing substantially more than she has been receiving, the relationship can quickly weaken. However, when there is a balanced reward system between people, the working relationship can thrive. The cases of Gabriella and Molly illustrate this theory.

Gabriella was a quiet, timid, serious worker with outstanding job knowledge. Joseph, on the other hand, was a very outgoing person with great personal confidence but with less job knowledge. They worked next to each other in identical jobs and, despite their differences, they slowly built a strong relationship.

How did it happen? Gabriella made a patient effort to teach Joseph as much as possible about the job and took care of some mistakes he made without the supervisor finding out about them. What did Joseph do in return? He helped Gabriella develop more self-confidence and become a more outgoing personality. He did this by paying her deserved compliments, introducing her to co-workers from other departments, and generally giving her a feeling of acceptance that she had not been able to develop by herself. Because each party contributed to the success of the other (both eventually became supervisors), their relationship became strong and permanent.

Molly worked for Ms. Gonzales for three years before taking over her job as department manager. During that period, MRT was constantly in effect. Molly provided high productivity, loyalty, and dependability to the department and to Ms. Gonzales. Ms. Gonzales, as supervisor, provided a good learning environment for Molly and gave her the recognition she needed. For example, Ms. Gonzales would often introduce Molly to upper-management people and relate the progress she was making. This exposure eventually gave Molly the edge she needed to achieve a promotion.

The term *bonding* is currently in popular use to signify a close, emotionally important relationship. In this context, bonding can take place between two co-workers, an employee and an immediate supervisor, and especially between an employee and a mentor. A working relationship that involves bonding needs to have two characteristics. First, it is important that the relationship not become overly personal to the point that present productivity and the future career of either individual is placed in jeopardy. Second, it is vital to the longevity of the relationship that it be mutually rewarding so that both parties benefit somewhat equally.

Relationships can almost always be mutually rewarding because people can strengthen each other in many different ways. Obviously, however, when one person does all the giving, deterioration quickly sets in. As you build new relationships and protect old ones, look for things you can do to contribute to the success and happiness of the person next to you. When you do this you will almost always receive something in return that will make life better for you. If you weave MRT into your behavior, you are demonstrating a significant human-relations competency.

Value Conflicts

Everyone has his or her own value system. Everyone has his or her own priority list of what is really important in life. Different people seek different lifestyles. Because of this, it is only natural that value conflicts exist between people who are forced to associate with each other closely in the world of work. Here are two typical examples.

Tony was assigned to work next to Mr. Henderson, who was more than twice his age. Tony was a bachelor who enjoyed an active social life and did not want to assume family responsibilities too soon in life. Tony was determined to come up with a lifestyle different from that of his parents. His foreign sports car and fashionable clothing reflected this attitude. Mr. Henderson, on the other hand, was a family-oriented, religious person.

How did they learn to work together gracefully? At the beginning they both played it cool and built their relationship exclusively on job factors. Tony learned to respect Mr. Henderson for his many years of job experience and his willingness to share it. Mr. Henderson learned to respect Tony for his willingness to learn and contribute a full day's work. After six months they could even discuss their value differences. A better mutual understanding was brought about.

Beverly was brought up in a strict home environment and was taught to respect discipline. She was considered fairly square by her contemporaries. Trish, on the other hand, was very happy-go-lucky and undisciplined. She considered herself very much ahead of others of her generation. How did Beverly and Trish get along when they were forced to work very closely with each other? At first the sparks of conflict were rather obvious. But slowly they built a sound working relationship based upon their mutual desire to do a good job for the company and further their careers. They did not become close personal friends, and they did not go out together socially. However, they learned to respect each other, and both benefited from the working relationship despite their value differences.

It is a mistake, perhaps even an invasion of privacy, to impose one's own personal values on another, especially in the work environment. What a fellow worker does with her private life is her own business and should have nothing to do with the relationship you build with her on the job. To react to an individual in a negative way for what she does on the outside should be avoided. Common interests on the job should provide enough of a basis for a good working relationship. You will be surprised how many good working relationships you can build with people who think and live differently than you do.

Ethnic Implications

Years ago white males were dominant in numbers and positions of authority in most organizations. Today there is more diversity at all levels. Some firms employ more women than men with increasing numbers in executive roles; others employ more Black and Hispanic people than whites; still others employ a high percentage from Asian and other cultures. Depending upon the "mix" within your organization, you can react in three different ways.

1. If you are in the "dominant" culture, you can maintain a negative attitude toward those in others. Those who do this rarely learn to work with others successfully and their careers suffer.

2. If you are in a "minority" culture, you can try so hard to be one of "them" that you lose your own identity at great expense to your own positive attitude and job productivity.

3. Regardless of the position you occupy, if you adapt to all cultures in your organization you will become a better person to know, you will be more productive, and your career will be enhanced.

A major attitude change is taking place in the United States. When our country was young, many people thought that we would become one culture with a single language and concentrate 100 percent on our own traditions. It didn't happen that way. Today, instead of being a great "melting pot," we are more like a "great mosaic" created out of different cultures.

Accepting this "international" or "mosaic" view may assist you in building strong and lasting relationships with all the many different people you will meet in your workplace. It will also help you maintain your positive attitude.

A basic human-relations competency is to respect and treat everyone as a unique and special individual. Look beyond out-

ward appearances, ignore how he or she might resemble someone you had an unfavorable experience with in the past, and accept each person for himself alone. If everyone could sincerely
adhere to this one fundamental practice, relationships would have a
good chance of functioning harmoniously. Each person — and
each relationship — would stand on its own without reference to
ethnic background. Unfortunately for all of us, not enough
people practice this principle. Here are two short cases to illustrate the point.

Although she had always believed she was free of prejudice, Jean had
very little close contact with blacks. She was therefore a little uneasy
about working closely with a Black person for the first time. Hobart,
a young Black, joined the department and, after introductions,
Jean's uneasiness gave way to anticipation. Hobart was a very easygoing, friendly guy. He would be fun to work with.

Everything went well as far as their relationship was concerned
until Hobart started to make a number of mistakes. He kept asking
what Jean felt were stupid questions and, in general, he did not live
up to her expectations. Jean became so frustrated over the matter
that she was tempted to go to her supervisor.

Then, all of a sudden, it came to her that she was expecting more
of Hobart because he was Black. She was looking for things to complain about instead of being understanding, as she would normally
be with a white person. Jean decided to get the relationship back on
a fair footing, so she invited Hobart for coffee and admitted her mistake. It was a good move because Hobart had felt Jean's negative attitude and wanted to build a better relationship himself.

Fernando and Archie were assigned two months ago to work as a
team on a moving van. Archie had graduated from a community college and hoped eventually to get into management. Fernando was a
high school graduate with over three years' experience in the furni-
ture-moving business.

Archie learned quickly that Fernando was an outstanding worker
with excellent skills. He also learned in a hurry that Fernando was
not much of a talker. In fact, Fernando only communicated when it
was necessary to get the job done.

This silence soon got on Archie's nerves. After making many attempts to get a light conversation going, he decided that Fernando
had a lot of deep-seated hostility toward Anglos. It was a very uncomfortable situation and because Archie needed to talk, he soon became a little bitter about the situation. Should he ask for a transfer?
Should he resign?

Then one day it occurred to him that, with a few beers, Fernando might open up and they could learn to communicate. He invited Fernando to be his guest, and they went to a place close to Fernando's home. It was a small place that reflected the Chicano culture. Sure enough, it wasn't long before Fernando felt sufficiently comfortable to start talking.

Archie learned a great deal. Fernando had been pushed around by many people. He did not feel accepted. His silence was more a defense than anything else. But what got to Archie was the fact that Fernando felt that Archie was against *him*, and not the other way around.

It was a revelation for both parties, and much of the tension that had been present on the job was gone the next day. Archie and Fernando had learned how to communicate. As a result, they started to work much better as a team. They didn't become personal friends, but they gained a high degree of mutual respect.

There are many relationships ahead of you that will involve people from different ethnic backgrounds. These relationships will not always be easy to build and maintain. Sometimes they may demand more perception than you possess. Yet, if you are open, honest, sincere, and willing to talk, your chances of building sound MRT relationships are excellent. In doing this, it is good to keep in mind that discussions of religious, political, and cultural differences do not belong in the workplace. If you judge others in ways they do not wish to be judged, they may do the same to you.

Sexual Overtones

Working relationships between employees frequently contain sexual overtones. For the most part, this sexual tension is not dangerous and has little important influence on productivity one way or the other. But not always. Take the case of Judy.

Judy was attracted sexually to her supervisor from the moment he was transferred into her department. A perceptive observer would have noticed that the very next day she started wearing the best clothes in her wardrobe. She became more particular with her makeup. She started working harder to win the favor of her new boss and to create more opportunities to talk with him on business matters.

So what happened? The other women in Judy's department

quickly sensed the sexual overtones to the relationship, and their positive attitude toward Judy began to cool. They became more distant, less willing to help her, and less tolerant of her mistakes. It didn't take long for a certain strain to develop among all the employees in the department, and productivity began to suffer.

Judy's case raises a very difficult question: *What are the human-relations dangers involved in dating someone where you work?*

There is little danger involved, provided the individual is not your supervisor, he or she works in a section separated from yours, and you are smart enough to keep your business and personal worlds separate. Under these circumstances, management will probably be very understanding.

There are some real dangers that you should know about in advance. However, most of them occur under the following circumstances: (1) when a supervisor dates someone in his or her own department, immediate cries of favoritism are raised and productivity is hurt; (2) when two people — especially if they are in the same section — date and do not keep their business and personal worlds separate, relationships with others are hurt and eventually productivity is lowered; and (3) when one or both parties are married, a sticky situation is created that can produce harmful gossip, hurt productivity, and sometimes make it necessary for management to step in.

Before you create or accept a dating situation where you work, you should also consider the chance of a breakup between the two of you at a later date. This could hurt both people involved and leave bad feelings among fellow employees who were in on the matter and took sides.

It is also important to keep in mind that sexual harassment from either men or women is now against the law in the work environment. This includes unsolicited touching, the use of suggestive language, and the telling of inappropriate sex-related stories. Obviously, dealing with sexual overtones in the workplace is a human-relations skill.

As you make your move to enhance your career, you will have more and more opportunities to build strong and satisfying MRT relationships at all levels and in many different situations, thus demonstrating your new competency in human relations.

Age Differences

The new employee who is young, capable, and ambitious is faced with a peculiar challenge in most organizations. And it doesn't take long for the challenge to present itself. You hear it expressed in many ways:

"I could have had that last promotion if I had had more seniority."

"Everyone in this outfit has age, seniority, or experience beyond mine. I'll never get a chance." "I'm wasting my time and ability. I won't get a chance to show what I can do until I'm thirty."

"I think I'll grow a mustache, so that I'll at least appear older."

Many employees between the ages of eighteen and thirty consider their youth a handicap. Some feel that they must put in time to reach a certain age level before they will be given a chance to demonstrate their ability. In a few cases the situation becomes aggravated because the employee appears younger than he or she actually is.

It is easy to appreciate this attitude if you put yourself in the place of a young employee. He or she sees older, more experienced employees all around. He may begin to feel the generation gap is wider inside a business organization than outside. Yet he wants to make progress. He wants to move. He doesn't want to wait. So the pressure builds.

Yet, it is not unusual today to find young supervisors in charge of employees many years their senior. Apparently some young people have the human-relations skills to compensate for their youth. Take the cases of Laurel and Leonard as examples.

Laurel manages a large fashion department in a major department store. The department had sales of over $1 million last year. Laurel supervises nine full-time people, all of whom are at least twice her age, which is twenty. The problems are constant and the pressure is great. But, without exception, the older workers consider her an excellent manager and her boss feels she has a great future.

Leonard, who is just twenty-three and has only one year of college behind him, is the manager of a large popular restaurant. Two of the three managers who work under him are much older than he, and one is old enough to be his father. As a matter of fact, most of the regular employees are older. The establishment is open twenty-four hours a day, and the problems never end. Yet Leonard seems to be on top of everything, and the president of the chain feels that he is just getting started.

How do young people like Laurel and Leonard do it?

They demonstrate early that they can accept and handle responsibility. They demonstrate that they can make mature decisions. They demonstrate great personal confidence. But most of all they demonstrate skills in human relations. They show that they can build strong MRT relationships with older and more experienced employees and management personnel, as well as with people their own age. The fact is that your more mature fellow workers will not resist personal progress if you go about it in the right way. Rather, they will want you to succeed and be willing to help you.

Your decision, then, is a simple one. If you are ambitious, you can either drift along until you are older and have more experience, or you can face the human-relations challenge now and speed up your progress. If you decide to make the effort, there are, among others, two important rewards you should provide in building a relationship with a more mature, experienced person.

Everyone, regardless of age, likes to be noticed. This is especially true of older employees. They like to receive compliments (even if the compliments border on flattery). They like to feel that they are still important as employees and as people. They need to feel appreciated and respected. They like to receive credit when due.

The more mature person often likes to keep a young image. Any action that tends to make a mature person feel out-of-touch or out-of-date is a mistake. Try to make him (or her) feel that he still has a lot to offer, that he is part of today's world, not yesterday's. Make a big effort to keep the communication lines open at all times. Do not isolate yourself from this person. Seek his advice. Always include him in your plans for any job-related social activities. Remember, you cannot expect a good vertical relationship with him — should you become his supervisor later on — unless you build a good horizontal working relationship with him now.

Perhaps the most important aspect of building good relationships with mature employees is learning how to gain their respect. This is usually done through ability, hard work, reliability on a day-today basis. Deeds will do more than words. Statistics will do more than promises. Performance will do more than flattery.

More than anything else, learn from this person. Her (or his) additional years of experience have taught her many things that you can learn without having to experience them. You can learn through osmosis. Then, if the time comes for you to move ahead of her, give her credit for making it possible. Let her have the satisfaction of calling you her protégée. Let her take pride in your success.

It will be wise of you to keep your relationship on a formal basis until she gives you the signal to be more relaxed and personal.

What about reversing the situation? How can the mature worker build better relationships with the new, younger employee? There are many steps that can be taken. Here are three that will be greatly appreciated: (1) be patient with new employees' adjustment problems, (2) help them learn by sharing your experience with them, and (3) if needed, give them the confidence to communicate with you.

Irritation Threshold

Relationships are frequently endangered because one of the individuals has an irritating habit or mannerism that bothers the other. Here are some common ones.

- Harsh or loud voice
- Irritating laugh
- Overbearing manner
- Constant name dropping
- Constant talk about money
- Constant reference to sex
- Telling dirty or unfunny stories
- Overuse of certain words or expressions
- Constant discussion of personal problems

- Constant complaining

- Constant bragging about their successes off the job or the successes of their children

Whether or not a habit or mannerism becomes an irritant depends upon the threshold or *tolerance level* of the second party. If one party has a high enough threshold, he or she may not even notice something that might bother someone else. On the other hand, it is possible for an individual to have a very low threshold for a certain mannerism, in which case the habit can do considerable damage to the relationship.

> Diane is an excellent example of a young employee who hurt her relationship with a few fellow workers because of a nervous giggle that followed almost every sentence she uttered. Unfortunately, Diane had no idea what was happening. She was not conscious of the habit or of the fact that it was hurting her relationships with certain people who had low irritation thresholds. One day, after getting a complaint from a good employee who worked next to Diane, the supervisor had a talk with her about it and, thanks to some very hard work on Diane's part, the irritating mannerism all but disappeared in a few weeks.

Once the individual knows about them, bad habits can usually be modified and sometimes eliminated. But the person at the other end of the relationship must not expect too much too soon. In some cases it may be necessary to learn to live with certain irritants by making an attempt to raise one's tolerance level. Seldom do such irritants come from only one side of the relationship. Almost all of us have at least a few mannerisms or habits that bother other people. The individual, even in the business environment, retains the right to remain pretty much the way he or she is, so some adjustment on your part to such factors will be necessary in most relationships. Tolerance, obviously, is a human-relations skill that must be developed.

Problem 8

CURRENCY

"What's in it for me?"

When it comes to his career, Sam deals in only one currency, and that is money. Sam wants "big bucks" and he wants them fast. Human relations and compassion (other forms of exchange) have no appeal to Sam.

You can read Sam's attitude in his movements. He appears totally confident and he seems to know how to be aggressive at just the right time. As a result, many of his classmates envy him for the job opportunities that he is bound to have offered to him.

A quiet dissenter is Ralph. Ralph feels that money is important but that it comes to those who select careers that contribute to the lives of others as much as to those who take a direct mega-bucks approach. Ralph made this comment to Sam (a good friend of his) yesterday: "You're going to make it fast, Sam, but I think I will be happier getting to where I'm going. And, who knows, I might wind up with as much money as you while my personal values remain intact. I think you are sacrificing human-relations values for the dollar, and in real life this is not necessary."

Sam replied: "It's a jungle out there, Ralph. You may wind up as happy as I do. But you and your values will get pushed around so much that you will be sidelined as far as money is concerned. I can worry about values after I have it made!"

How would you reply if you were part of the above conversation? Would you side with Sam or Ralph? How do you intend to maintain your personal values and still enjoy monetary success? (For a suggested answer, see page 190).

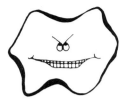

"1 2 3 4 5 6 ..."

CHAPTER **9**

RELEASING YOUR FRUSTRATIONS HARMLESSLY

This chapter has one simple goal and that is to introduce you to the *frustration-aggression hypothesis*. It is an idea that can greatly help you understand your own behavior, as well as that of others. Here is the story.

Everyone encounters frustrations in life. We learn to adjust to most of them easily, without hurting our relations with others. Sometimes, however, a major frustration or series of frustrations may cause our feelings to boil to the point where we lash out verbally and seriously injure or destroy a relationship we deeply treasure.

Naturally there are many experiences that occur on the job that are disturbing. In fact, most of your frustrations may be job-oriented. The mechanic who climbs under a car to do a repair job—only to discover that he (or she) took the wrong wrench with him—becomes frustrated. A supervisor who must get a report in before going home to an important dinner engagement must deal with feelings of frustration.

A frustration is the inner feeling of disturbance or anxiety you experience when you meet a temporary block to your immediate goal.

The more important the goal is to you, the more intense is the disturbance. Major frustrations come about when something happens to keep you from reaching a goal that means a great deal to you. While small frustrations can usually be dealt with quickly, major frustrations must often be controlled for days or weeks before an adjustment can be made. This often means replacing one goal with another.

Now we must ask ourselves the big question: What happens when we become frustrated?

Almost always we become aggressive. When a steam boiler builds up too much pressure inside, some of the steam must be released. If there is no safety valve, the boiler will explode. Just as the steam boiler must release some of the pressure after it reaches a certain point, so must the individual. This release usually comes in some form of aggressive behavior.

Take the case of the driver who becomes frustrated when he (or she) meets a slow-moving car on the highway. He may curse (verbal aggression) and drive on. Or he may pound his horn and speed around the slow car (physical aggression). Or it could disturb him so much that when he returns to his office he may refuse to speak to his secretary or co-workers (passive aggression).

Aggression takes many forms. Physical aggression, especially if it involves another person, is serious. It can be assault and battery and could mean a police record. Verbal aggression can also get a person into serious trouble. Telling off a fellow worker or supervisor at the wrong time and wrong place can destroy a relationship and cripple a person's progress.

The idea is to learn to release our aggression in acceptable ways without hurting our relationships with others. There are acceptable forms of physical aggression. There are acceptable forms of verbal aggression.

A parent might become frustrated because of her (or his) small children. She could act out the aggression that follows the frustration by punishing one child with a very harsh slap in the face. This is an unacceptable release of aggression. On the other hand, if the parent released her aggression physically, by energetically washing windows, and then disciplined the child in some other manner, it would be more acceptable. This way the mother is taking out her aggression on the windows — not on the child.

There are many acceptable ways a person can release inner tension due to frustrations. Here are a few.

ON THE JOB	OFF THE JOB
Take a walk	Cook exotic foods
Talk things over with a third party	Clean out the garage
	Play golf or go bowling
Do some disagreeable stock work	

Sometimes just by doing something physical we release inner tensions and no one is hurt. It is usually more difficult to find acceptable ways to release inner tensions on the job than it is off the job.

If a worker became frustrated on the job and picked a fight with a fellow worker, this would be an unacceptable release of aggression. If, on the other hand he (or she) released his aggressions by walking away and slamming a door where nobody could hear it, he would be releasing his aggression in an acceptable manner. He *could* hurt his human relationships, however, by slamming a door in *front* of others. They might interpret the action as a display of temper or immaturity.

As a mature, mentally healthy person, you must seek and find acceptable releases for your inner aggression. You should conduct yourself in such a manner as to eliminate many of the frustrations of life. The fewer frustrations you have, the fewer times you will have to seek acceptable releases.

But you cannot eliminate all frustrations from life. You should expect to find it necessary to release your anxiety feelings occasionally. It is not always healthy for a person to keep his or her inner tensions bottled up inside. Some release is necessary and healthy. You will do well, however, to refrain from any kind of verbal aggression on the job. It would be wiser to unburden yourself to someone you can trust outside the organization — your spouse or a good friend.

Here is an illustration that will help you to understand the importance of the frustration-aggression hypothesis.

Alice was intelligent, highly motivated, and well educated. She joined a large utility company as a management trainee. She liked her job, and for two years her productivity and human relations were very good. She took advantage of every opportunity to learn. She received four salary increases.

One day, in talking to the director of human resources she mentioned that she would like to qualify as an employment interviewer. The director, pleased with her success so far, encouraged her. He told Alice that she would be considered if an opportunity came along. Alice, more highly motivated than ever, continued to do an outstanding job and set her goal for the next opening as an interviewer.

Two weeks later another person was promoted to the position of interviewer. Alice was not informed about the change. Not thinking that the plans for this personnel change might have been set before her initial talk with the director, Alice permitted herself to become deeply frustrated. She had set a goal for herself and now they had selected another person.

"At least they could have talked to me!"

"Why should that person get the breaks?"

"So that's the way they keep their promises!"

Alice, without thinking it through, permitted her frustration to grow. Indeed, she set out to feed it, for talking it over with a few fellow employees only intensified her feelings.

What happened?

Alice released her frustrations through verbal aggression. For the first time in her career, she sounded off in a highly emotional manner at a weekly staff meeting. She voiced more than her share of gripes during coffee breaks. And all of this found its way back to the Department of Human Resources. What was the result? What you might expect: Alice, through her verbal aggression, had hurt her previously excellent relationships with others. Six months later another position as an interviewer opened up, and Alice was passed over.

What should she have done?

Alice should have released her aggressive behavior outside her job until she discovered the truth of the situation. She could have spent more time playing her favorite sport or talking her problem over with a close friend. Or she could have put it into writing without showing it to others. This seems to help a number of people. None of these actions would have injured human relations with others.

We must all learn to live with frustrating experiences without becoming verbally aggressive on the job, without damaging our relations with others, *without victimizing ourselves*.

Aggressive behavior coming from inner disturbances and hostilities takes many strange forms. It's not always physical or verbal. It may be passive. In extreme cases, passive aggression takes the form of silence. Deliberate silence. Planned silence.

Silence on the part of the person who has been frustrated is a most potent weapon. Nothing is more uncomfortable to your fellow workers than your silence. Nothing destroys relations faster. No one can interpret your silence. All anyone can do is leave you alone and wait. But it is uncomfortable for them, and productivity suffers.

When a person takes out his or her inner aggressive feelings in silence, who is at the receiving end? Fellow employees? The supervisor? Although everyone suffers from silence of this nature, the silent person himself suffers the most. He is, in fact, taking out his aggressive feelings on himself. It is a form of self-victimization. Naturally this is most destructive to the human personality. It is also juvenile. Many normal, mature people, however, temporarily react to a series of frustrations in this manner.

It is hoped that the preceding discussion has given the reader a good understanding of the frustration-aggression hypothesis. To summarize, how can you put this idea to work for you?

1. If you really understand the idea, you will admit that your frustrations often produce aggressive behavior of some kind and you should learn to recognize it. With this recognition should come the ability to channel aggressive actions into acceptable outlets. Be careful to release your aggressions in the right way and in the right place. Keep from releasing them on the job in a way that will hurt relationships and your future.

2. You should be able to recognize aggressive behavior in others (including executives). This should help you remember that aggressive action by others is usually not directed toward you personally. You may just happen to be at the wrong place at the wrong time and the best available target for verbal abuse. You should try to accept such behavior as a natural outcome of uncontrollable frustrations and not overreact to it. This attitude should make for better human understanding. Your relationship with this person will not suffer as much.

3. You should be more sensitive to verbal aggression on your own part and be very cautious in group discussions and staff meetings. When you need to release feelings verbally, do so to a friend outside the company and not to a fellow employee, thus protecting your work relationships.

4. You should not let aggressive behavior keep you from reaching your ultimate goal. When a detour is necessary, you should take it. When an unexpected block to your plans appears, accept it for what it is. If frustration occurs, release it in acceptable ways and come up with an alternate goal. Do not allow aggressive behavior to victimize you on a permanent basis.

There is another form of aggression that should be mentioned. It is subtle and sinister and has been the downfall of many career-minded persons. It is aggression on the part of an employee toward the company for which he or she works. There is rarely anything personal about such a person's aggressive behavior. Such a person seems to get along well enough with his fellow workers and immediate supervisors. Instead, his aggression always seems to be directed toward the company itself. It isn't just the top brass or middle management. It is the company. He often seems to hold his present plight (lack of progress or of personal adjustment to life) against the company.

In a very real sense it is frustrating to work inside any organization. Some rules must be followed. Some degree of conformity is expected. Some loss of individuality is usually necessary. Some people, however, seem to nurse their minor frustrations into one major hang-up against the organization itself. When this is permitted to happen, aggressive action of serious proportions frequently develops. The employee begins to fight a hypothetical monster that seems to be controlling his life without giving him a chance to change. Often one hears expressions like these from such an individual:

"This outfit does nothing but chew people up and spit them out."

"This company is so large that the only thing that keeps us from getting lost altogether is the computer."

"I'd put in for a transfer but by the time it got through channels I'd be ready to retire.

It is counterproductive to direct one's aggressive behavior toward a large corporate structure. In the first place, these organizations are usually too large. Second, when a person attacks his company, he starts to lose loyalty to it. *And it begins to show in his attitude* — not overnight, of course, but in subtle ways that begin to hurt that person's progress in the company.

This chapter has attempted to show you why you should try to release your frustrations harmlessly. Its purpose has been to help you avoid self-victimization so that you maintain the kind of positive, productive relationships that will further, not hinder, your career progress.

Problem 9

FRUSTRATION

"Me and my big mouth!"

It took Victor three months to make up his mind to switch to the new company. His decision to do so was based primarily upon the promise that they would push him ahead as fast as possible. In his opinion his previous firms had never given him the opportunity to move ahead at a pace that was satisfying to him.

Shortly before Vic had completed six months with the company, he was asked if he would accept a transfer to another plant some 200 miles away. He immediately interpreted this to mean he was getting a big promotion. He accepted and became very excited about the move.

On reporting to work at the new plant, however, he discovered he had little more responsibility than at the one he had left. There was no discussion of a pay increase. Having built up his hopes, Vic felt let down.

Then other things happened. He soon learned that his living expenses were higher in the new location. His wife told him that the schools there were not as good. One negative thing after another happened until Vic became increasingly frustrated. One afternoon, after two weeks in the new assignment, he walked into the office of his supervisor and explosively released his pent-up feelings.

Halfway through the outburst his superior said, "Slow down. Take it easy. Cool off. Relax." Then he proceeded to read a letter just received from the home office announcing that Vic was to replace a man who had just received a promotion himself. It was a big jump.

Was Vic justified in his outburst? What might he have done to prevent it? Did he harm himself permanently, even though he did receive the promotion? (For a suggested answer, see page 190.)

CHAPTER 10

"Some relationships
are not worth saving."

RESTORING INJURED RELATIONSHIPS

No matter how skillful one becomes at building healthy and rewarding human relationships, such relationships can easily be damaged through insensitivity and misunderstanding by either party. Human relationships are fragile. Once an injury occurs, the restoration process can be like walking on glass barefooted; it can be difficult — even challenging — but not impossible.

In the work environment, damages occur when there is a misuse of power by leaders, when the behavior of one party with another is less than honest, when there are breakdowns in communications, and for a host of other reasons, many of which are highly personal and unintended. The important thing to remember is that *all* relationships — both on and off the job — occasionally become damaged and need repairing. When repair work is required and nothing is done about it, everyone loses. That is why it could be to your advantage to initiate restoration *even when you are not primarily responsible for the injury.*

Without intending to do so, June let her emotions spill over last Friday and became testy with Grace — her favorite co-worker. Grace, wounded emotionally, reacted with a huffy silence for the rest of the day. June worried about that situation all weekend but failed to make repairs Monday. Early Tuesday, Grace initiated a discussion on the incident which gave June an opportunity to apologize, and the relationship was restored. Although she was not at fault, Grace was not content to work under an uncomfortable climate, so she used her human-relations skills to restore the relationship.

Last week Gilbert came down too hard on Harry over a minor work rule infraction. Harry, knowing Gilbert (his supervisor) would find it difficult to apologize, took action himself. On the following day he said: "Gilbert, our relationship is important to me, so I want to keep communication lines open and eliminate any differences that may occur between us. I want to be relaxed and comfortable under your supervision. Is it a deal?"

Unfortunately, when a minor falling-out between two people occurs, both parties may have a desire to "nurse the hurt" and pull farther away from each other. If this is allowed to continue, some dangerous side effects may develop. For example, the possibility exists that the relationship between them may become more "toxic" and spill over into relationships with others.

The rift that developed between Jill and Jessie pushed Jill into a negative rut where some of her other relationships seemed to turn sour. The cause? A change in attitude. Jill started to ask herself such questions as: "Why should I work hard to build healthy relationships when others could care less?" "Why should I permit myself to be vulnerable to the hurts others carelessly impose upon me?" Result? Jill withdrew into her newly designed shell and became less of a team member on the job and less socially accepted in her personal world. Jill had made the classic human relations mistake of permitting a repairable rift to develop into a major problem.

If communication is the lifeblood of any relationship (see Chapter 8, page 68), then reopening communication lines should be the first step in restoring relationships. Which party initiates the communication is unimportant. Communication, in this sense, can be compared to using ointment to help heal a cut. The ointment (communication) by itself may not solve the problem, but it enhances the healing process. If neither party is willing to supply or apply the ointment, the wound may fester and eventually destroy the relationship.

Regardless of who may be at fault (often both parties are responsible), it is effective human-relations practice to restore the relationship *as soon as possible*. Any lapse of time may seem to deaden the pain, but it can make restoration more difficult — and sometimes impossible. And those who move from one job to another, leaving a wake of broken relationships behind them, often pay a high price in many directions. Consider the following possibilities.

Loss of constructive "mind-time." Preoccupation with a relationship left unrepaired is self-defeating. Living day in and day out with an unhealthy relationship, especially with a supervisor, causes you to "mentally reprocess" the conflict over and over, thus stealing your "mind-time" from more constructive pursuits. Those who permit this to happen often put their career progress on hold or in jeopardy.

Compounds an already stressful situation. Emotional conflicts in the workplace can be more stressful than long hours, heavy concentration on a special project, or other heavy job demands. Worst of all, emotional stress makes everything else more difficult. To maintain peace of mind and high personal productivity, restoration of broken relationships should receive top priority. When this is not the case, false inferences often compound the stress. For years statistics have indicated that over 50 percent of all resignations come from unsolved human conflicts.

Chances of becoming a victim increase. In some work environments, a broken relationship left unattended can convert you into a victim. For example, a co-worker, with whom you have previously enjoyed a healthy relationship, suddenly begins to fear you may replace him or her. As a result, this individual deliberately creates a conflict situation in the hope you cannot deal with it effectively. If the supervisor does not step in as a mediator/counselor, and you refuse to take action yourself, you could easily wind up a victim. Your refusal to take action (even going to the supervisor with the problem) could give the co-worker the upper hand he or she seeks, and eventually management could misinterpret the situation in favor of the other party. Your failure to remove the feeling of fear through communication and restore the relationship to its previous state could cause you to become a victim.

Such possibilities, although remote, should motivate you to set the difficult goal of creating, maintaining, and *repairing* relationships, even when you would prefer to ignore the individuals involved or carry out a vendetta against them. In some cases your career may depend upon how effective you are.

There are four principles or guideposts that may assist you in repairing a damaged relationship.

1. See the connection between repairing relationships and career success. A damaged relationship left unrepaired between you and a co-worker or superior may reduce support you need at a later date. As a result, your upward mobility may be impeded. You have victimized yourself.

2. Try to see behind the cause of the falling out. When one takes the time to study the causes of "breaks" in human relationships, it becomes obvious that often one party was under unusual pressure, which precipitated the rift. It is easier to "forgive" when such causes can be identified. Through your own perception, try to see behind misunderstandings. Once you see *why* they occur, your attitude toward rebuilding them may be more positive.

3. Develop a willingness to rebuild damaged relationships. The more you nurse a resentment, the less effective you are when it comes to the restoration of a relationship. Some give and take from both ends is usually necessary for a satisfactory repair job. If one party is unwilling to listen, the process may never get off the ground. That is why some relationships are never repaired. Until you reach a point where your mind is open to the possibility of repair (regardless of who did the damage), you have not reached the effective level of *willingness*.

4. Design your own rebuilding techniques. As you ponder just *how* you might initiate a rebuilding process, many questions will emerge in your mind. Can both parties "save face"? If hostility and resentment are present, can they be dissipated through open communication so that the repair job is permanent? As you consider such factors, ask yourself these additional questions.

Can you insert some humor into your approach?

Can you be a better listener than talker?

Can you "give" as much as you expect from the other party?

Can you forgive a "little white lie" so that the other party can "save face?"

Are you willing to state openly that the relationship is important to you—important enough to forgive and forget what or who caused the damage?

Once you feel your "willingness factor" is sufficient, consider these rebuilding strategies.

Rebuilding strategy #1: If you were fully or partially responsible for the damage, swallow your pride and take the direct approach. Say you are sorry and state: "I would like to get our relationship back to its previous healthy state as soon as possible. You and our relationship are important to me, and I intend to be more sensitive in the future."

We all make human-relations mistakes. We always will. Unless we accept the premise that now and then we need to initiate a "repair job," we will lose many significant relationships well worth keeping.

Rebuilding strategy #2: When the party at the other end of the relationship line makes the mistake (the reason is not important), give that party the opportunity to approach you to restore the relationship. Be accessible! Have an open mind! If the party does not approach you in a reasonable length of time, take the initiative yourself. This may sound like asking too much, but keep in mind that you may be getting hurt more than the person responsible. Why should you become a victim? Why not restore the relationship for *your* benefit? One way to employ strategy #2 is to say: "That incident last week really got to me, Jack, and I'm bringing it up for discussion so that it hopefully won't happen again. If we don't work harder at maintaining our relationship, we will both wind up losers."

Rebuilding Strategy #3: When no one is clearly responsible for a rift, initiate an MRT discussion so that the rewards parties are receiving from the relationship can be reviewed. This approach can help each party recognize how important the relationship has been in the past and can continue to be in the future. Only when rewards are somewhat equal do both parties come out ahead. That is the significance and the promise of MRT.

Restoring a damaged relationship involves risks. You may, for example, gather up your courage in a sincere effort to restore an important relationship only to be rebuffed for your initiative.

After two days of increased silence and tension on the job, Howard approached his boss to reconcile a communications misunderstanding. His boss responded by walking away. However, the following morning Howard's boss invited him to lunch, and the relationship was fully restored. With time to think over Howard's gesture, his boss had a change of attitude. The risk had been worth taking after all.

Some people refuse to restore a relationship even if the alternative means finding a new job. Yet the challenge of restoration can be rich and rewarding and, at times, can give a career a needed boost.

In conclusion, keep in mind that a professional technician needs just the right tool to repair a sensitive instrument. The right tool to repair a damaged relationship is communication — in fact, it is the *only* tool available. When you use communication in a sensitive manner, you will be more than pleased with your repair jobs.

Problem 10

Restoration

"I'm willing if you are."

A few weeks ago Mr. Sisco, a highly respected supervisor, was asked by his superior to find and train a replacement for himself. Recognizing that a promotion was in the wind for him, Mr. Sisco interviewed over a dozen prospects. He was in the process of recommending Mrs. Peal, when management assigned him a young man named Dennis as the replacement.

Although the experience was upsetting to Mr. Sisco, he proceeded to devote all his spare time to training Dennis to the best of his ability. Despite all of Sisco's efforts to be skillful in building a healthy relationship, a serious conflict developed. Dennis seemed to ignore Mr. Sisco's suggestions and, at times, questioned his authority; he kept talking about needing "more freedom" to develop his own style. Soon the conflict was obvious to the rest of the staff, and productivity started to drop. Little communication was taking place between Mr. Sisco and Dennis. What chance is there that a healthy relationship can be restored? Who should initiate the process? What is the association in management's eyes between Mr. Sisco's readiness for advancement and his success with Dennis's readiness to replace him? (For a suggested answer, see page 191.)

PART III

BUILDING
YOUR CAREER

CHAPTER **11**

SUCCEEDING IN A NEW JOB OR ASSIGNMENT

Undoubtedly you want to succeed on any new job or assignment you undertake. First, you want to prove to your family, friends, and management that you are a winner. Second, you want to prove it to yourself. There is a great deal at stake.

This chapter is devoted to ten tips that can help you in reaching your goal. If you take these tips seriously and apply them conscientiously, you can avoid many of the mistakes others make.

Tip 1: Balance Home and Career

When you accept a new work challenge, it is vital that all home demands be under complete control. Your on-the-job concentration needs to be at a high level, and any home worries, especially those connected with small children or other relatives, can be distracting to both you and your co-workers. Balancing home and career, so that you can be a winner in both areas, is never easy to accomplish and maintain. The time to start (or reorganize) is *before* you accept a new job or assignment. Once things are out of balance, it may be too late for you to reach your full job potential. Give your career a break and get things organized at home *first*.

When it is necessary to call in ill, make every effort to talk to your supervisor or another management person. If a co-worker tells your boss you won't be in, doubts may be raised and your supervisor could call you for verification. Also, it never hurts to bring in a doctor's note to document an extended absence.

Tip 2: Take a Calendar Notebook to Work with You

An abundance of important information — rules, regulations, and procedures — will be thrown at you at the beginning of a new job. The first days are days of adjustment and excitement, so don't trust your mind to remember everything. Rather, buy yourself an inexpensive calendar notebook and use it to record some of the instructions and hard-to-remember information you get from your supervisor or fellow workers. Jot these data down in your notebook as they are being given to you.

Do not hesitate to take notes when receiving a complex answer to a question involving considerable detail. The notebook itself (if not overused) will create a good impression. It will help show that you are an organized person and are methodical in your approach to learning and serious about your career. In the evening, use it to review certain facts and procedures. You can also use it to record appointments, ideas, names, and so on.

Tip 3: Ask Questions, But Learn to Ask the Right Ones

Fear of being considered inadequate is the reason most people in a new work situation do not ask more questions. This is understandable, but it is better to ask questions than to suffer the serious results of continued mistakes. If you don't understand something, ask questions until you do. This may be necessary because those responsible for your adjustment and training do not always take enough time to explain things fully. Because old hands tend to forget that they, too, had trouble learning at the beginning, they often talk so fast that only a genius or a psychic could get the message the first time around.

There is a right and wrong time to ask a question. One should not, for example, interrupt a person who is concentrating on getting a job done or who is communicating with others. There are also right and wrong questions. A right question is one you need to ask to be effective; a wrong question is one that does not apply to the task being explained. One should not, for example, ask questions that are answered in the orientation literature you have been given to read on your own time.

In asking questions, keep in mind that you must listen to the answers with your eyes as well as your ears. Sure, you receive the auditory impressions with your ears. But you should also look at the person who is speaking. Most people, in fact, feel it is discourteous when someone they are talking to lets his or her eyes wander. You will understand this if you have ever seen someone look at his watch, shuffle papers, stare at the floor, or look out a window while you are talking to him. You will make a better impression on people if you form the habit of listening with your eyes as well as your ears. You also stand a better chance of receiving any hidden — but vital — meaning that may lie under the message.

Tip 4: Use Good Judgment in Working Extra Hours and Taking Your Breaks

Some employees with a new opportunity attempt to secure their jobs and attract management's attention by working more than the normal number of hours at the beginning. They arrive first in the morning and make a point of leaving last at the end of the day. They often skip their breaks. This attitude, if sincere, is to be admired.

However, overzealousness can get you into trouble on two counts. First, there are usually regulations governing hours to be worked. On certain jobs, unauthorized overtime work and failure to take breaks can involve you and your employer in labor difficulties. It is important, therefore, always to abide by the instructions given to you by management.

Second, your fellow employees may misinterpret your motives and make life more difficult for you and your supervisor. Working extra hours and eliminating breaks when an important deadline must be met and when you are asked to do it by your supervisor is one thing. Working extra hours only to impress others is quite another.

As a rule, it is better to make full use of the time you spend on the job, rather than to try to impress others with your willingness to work extra hours.

Many employees, especially those who are closely monitored by management, feel they need to immerse themselves in work as soon as they enter the workplace. It is often better to circulate around and send out a few friendly signals before digging in. Some people call this "doing a figure 8."

Tip 5: Don't Flaunt Your Education or Previous Experience

You may have had more formal education than many of the people you will work with on your new job. But these people probably have far more on-the-job experience and practical know-how than you do. That being the case, you would be wise to let them discover your educational background and experience gradually.

The job you are assigned may be more difficult than you expect. If you try to impress people with your experience or intelligence, they may not want to give you any help when you most need it.

If you are an experienced employee, you may have received your job training in another company. You will probably find that things are done differently in your new firm. Perhaps your way of doing things is better. But until you are sure, be safe and do it the way people at your new job do it. Give your co-workers the satisfaction of explaining how they do things. You will have plenty of time later to make changes that will be an improvement.

It is also a good idea to keep your salary to yourself. It is possible that another employee, doing work similar to what you are doing as you start out, has yet to reach your salary level. Misinterpretation and resentment might occur. If so, both you and the other employee could lose.

Tip 6: Make Friends, But Don't Make Close Friends Too Soon

There are many little human-relations traps you can easily fall into in a new work environment. One of these is building one or two very strong friendships at the expense of all others. For example, suppose you discover that one of the employees in your department is extremely friendly the first day. Such friendliness is usually more than welcome the first few hours in a strange setting.

But beware. What if you spend all your time with this one employee and neglect being friendly to the others? What if this friendly person is not respected by the others? What if he or she has earned a poor reputation in the department and is offering you friendship from purely selfish motives?

Sometimes people who have failed to earn respect from others at work try desperately to win the friendship of a new employee. Remember that it is only natural that the other employees (including management) will quickly identify you with any employee or employees with whom you spend excessive time.

If one employee clings to you as you start your new job, you obviously have a difficult situation to handle. Of course, you should not be rude to this person. You will do well, however, to back away and be somewhat reserved toward this individual for the first few weeks and concentrate on building relationships with everyone.

Tip 7: Look Energetic, But Don't Be an Eager Beaver

Some people start their careers with a great burst of energy and enthusiasm that cannot possibly be sustained. These people frequently create a favorable impression to begin with, but later on are reclassified by both management and their fellow workers.

It is easy to be overeager at the beginning. You are new to your job, so you have a fresh and dynamic approach. You have a great deal of nervous energy to release. You are interested, and your interest motivates you to achieve. This desire to succeed, however, might cause you to reach too far too fast.

The best way to make progress inside an organization is to make steady progress.

Goal setting is a good idea and may help you achieve an even work tempo. Daily goals, written down and accomplished according to a priority system, make you a more productive and valuable member of the team. The practice will also help you in preparing for a supervisory role.

Tip 8: Different Organizations Have Different Personal-Appearance and Grooming Standards

A few organizations, like factories, have no personal-appearance or grooming standards. They are interested primarily in your work performance and your human-relations ability.

Other companies, especially those that deal directly with customers, set minimum standards that are usually easy to live up to. Still other companies, like department stores, have rather high personal and grooming standards that may be difficult for some people to accept.

When you join an organization, you should carefully assess it and decide what is best for you and your future. You have a right to be yourself and protect your individuality. In doing so, however, you should weigh all factors and take into consideration that most people, including management, feel that a little conformity won't hurt you. You are responsible for meeting minimum dress standards. Managers quickly tire of those who try to slip by with unacceptable attire. They often interpret such behavior as immature.

Tip 9: Read Your Employee Handbook and Other Materials Carefully

Many organizations publish handbooks and other materials for their employees. These pamphlets usually contain vital information. Yet many employees, especially those with experience elsewhere, never read them.

Don't be casual in your use of company literature. Where else can you learn company policies that can keep you out of trouble? Where else can you discover important data that will prevent you from asking unnecessary questions? Take home all of the literature you are given and devote some time to it. Understanding your company and the benefits provided will not only help you start on the right foot, it will further your career.

Tip 10: Send Out Positive Verbal and Nonverbal Signals

There are many verbal signals you can use to create a good first impression. "Good morning" and "Thank you" are examples. Such easy signals of friendship should be transmitted at every opportunity to acknowledge the presence of others and to recognize any courtesies they have extended to you, however small.

A friendly person—one who creates a good first impression—is also one who uses nonverbal signals. For example, a person with a ready smile is easily interpreted as a friendly person. The smile seems to break any psychological barriers that might exist in a meeting of strangers. You immediately feel accepted by this person. A smile, then, is a friendly, nonverbal signal.

There are many effective nonverbal signals in addition to the smile. Shaking hands, gesturing positively with the hand or head, opening doors for people—these are all signals you send that make it easier for people to meet and know you. When you send out such signals naturally and in good taste, others do not feel awkward about approaching you. You have made it easy for them, and they like you for it.

In communicating a positive attitude to co-workers or clients, body language is most important. You probably have heard people say, "That's no problem," while their attitude (communicated through their body language) demonstrated that it was, indeed, a problem.

People who develop confidence in sending out such signals of friendship make excellent first impressions. They quickly increase their sphere of influence and build many lasting working and personal relationships. Have confidence in yourself and your ability to send out such signals. Take the initiative. Send out your own brand of signals in your own style, and be a comfortable person to meet.

Remember, too, that the better you become at this, the better prepared you will be for any job interviews you may face in the future.

Problem 11

Nonprofessional

"Whom can you trust?"

Thomas is normally an honest individual. He would never think of stealing office supplies for home use, for example, but he seems to feel ideas are open game. In practice, Thomas thinks nothing of embellishing an idea, created and introduced in casual conversation by another supervisor, and submitting it to his superior as if it were his own. Many of his written suggestions are ideas discussed informally and in confidence among co-workers in the organization.

Two weeks ago Helen shared a layout idea at an informal luncheon meeting where Thomas was present. Tuesday morning, after a discussion with their common supervisor, Helen discovered that Thomas had submitted her layout idea as his; as a result he will receive a commendation at this Friday's staff meeting.

If you were Helen, what would you do? Where does "ethics" (or ethical behavior) fit into the practice of human relations at work? (For a suggested answer, see page 192.)

12

INITIATION RITES — COPING WITH TEASING AND TESTING

Getting started in a new job or assignment, where the setting is strange and the employees are strangers, is bound to give you a few psychological challenges. It is not my purpose to magnify these. Rather, I wish to help you understand why such problems sometimes develop—and, even more important, show you how you can handle them.

You may be assigned to a department as a replacement for someone the others hated to lose. They will need time to get used to you. You may not have the experience of the person you replace, and as a result others may have to work harder for a few days to get you started. It is even possible that someone in your new department wanted another person to have your job, and there may be some resentment toward you because of this.

It is never easy to be the newest member of a group. You cannot expect to go from being an outsider to being an insider without making a few adjustments. In the first place, you and your personality were forced upon the group. They were not asked whether they wanted you. You have been, in effect, imposed upon them. Because they were there first, and because they probably have strong relationships among themselves, they may feel that you should earn your way into their confidence. It may not seem fair, but it is only natural for them to look at your arrival in this way.

Did you ever go through an initiation into a club? If so, you will understand that teasing or testing the new member is often traditional. To a limited extent, the same can be true when a new employee joins a department or division in a business organization. There is nothing planned or formal about it, of course, but you should be prepared for a little good-natured teasing or testing. Let us look at the psychological reasons behind these two phenomena.

The teasing of a new employee is often nothing more than a way of helping the person become a full-fledged member of the group. It is a form of initiation rite that will help you feel you belong. Sometimes it is a group effort in which everyone is in on the joke. More often, however, it is an individual matter.

Teasing, for the most part, is harmless.

The shop foreman who never had the advantage of a college education — but who has learned a great deal from practical experience — might enjoy teasing a recent graduate of an engineering school. If the graduate engineer goes along with the teasing, a sound relationship between the two should develop. If, however, she (or he) permits it to get under her skin, the relationship could become strained.

The shop foreman's motive might be nothing more than a desire to help the new engineer build good relationships with the rest of the gang. There may be nothing resentful or personal about it.

A small group of employees who work together closely in a branch bank, lawyer's office, or similar situation can usually be expected to come up with a little harmless teasing when a new person joins the staff. He might be given the oldest equipment with a touch of formal ceremony or the dismal job of keeping the stockroom in order.

Usually this kind of teasing is based upon tradition and human nature. People who like to tease in this manner are generally good-natured. They enjoy people. They mean no harm. In fact, they usually do it to make you feel more comfortable, not less.

If you are on the receiving end of some good, healthy teasing, you have nothing to worry about so long as you don't take it personally. Just go along with it and you'll come out ahead. It is much better to be teased than to be ignored. If by chance the baiting should go a little too far and you find yourself embarrassed, the very fact that it is embarrassing to you will probably make you some friends. In fact, you will be lucky if there is some mild hazing. It will help you get off to a good start. It will help break down any communications barriers that might exist.

Testing is different. It can have more serious implications. It will take more understanding on your part.

There are two kinds of testing. One is *organizational testing.* This kind comes from the organization (management, personnel, or your supervisor) and is a deliberate attempt to discover what kind of person you really are and whether you can adjust to certain conditions. The other kind comes strictly from individuals. This is *personal testing* — one person trying out another because of personality conflicts or inner prejudices.

Let's look at organizational testing first.

Almost all kinds of organizations — especially the smaller ones — have certain unpleasant tasks that must be done. Traditionally, these tasks are handed to the newest member. The new salesperson in a department store may be given excessive amounts of stock work at the start of his or her career. The factory worker may be given unpleasant cleanup jobs until another new member joins the department. The clerical employee may be given a nasty filing assignment to start with.

The important thing to recognize is that these tests have a purpose. Can the new worker take the assignment without complaining? Can he survive without developing a negative attitude? Or will he show resentment and thereby destroy his chance of gaining the respect of the other members of the department?

The old phrase "starting at the bottom of the ladder" sometimes means exactly that. Many top management people started at the bottom, and they feel that this is the best way for you to start. If you can't take it to begin with, you may not be able to assume heavy responsibility later. It is the price you pay for being a beginner.

Management sometimes feels that this is the best way for the manager of the future to appreciate fully the kind of work that must be done by the rank-and-file employee. Many a college graduate finds herself (or himself) doing the most uninviting tasks to start with. If she is human-relations smart, she will take it in stride, using the time to size up the situation and learn as much about the organization as possible.

During testing periods you are being watched by management and by your fellow employees. *The better you react, the sooner the testing will end and the better your relations with others will be.* In other words, although getting the job done is important, your attitude toward it may be more important. If you react in a negative manner, three things can happen: (1) you may be kept on the assignment longer that you otherwise would have been, (2) you may hurt your chances for a better assignment later on, and (3) you may damage relationships with people involved in or observing the testing.

If you can take the long-range perspective and condition yourself to these tasks with an inner smile and an outward grin, you'll do well for yourself. Roll up your sleeves and get the job done quickly. If you finish one job, move on to another. Don't be afraid to get dirty. If you must take a little abuse, don't complain. It is part of the initiation rite, and you will look back on it someday as those ahead of you look back on it now. It would be foolhardy for the new employee to fight any of the many forms of organizational testing, as long as it doesn't seriously damage his or her personal dignity.

Personal testing is a different matter. It could give you more trouble, especially if you fail to recognize it for what it is. It may come from someone your own age or someone much older or younger. It may come from a fellow worker or it may come from someone in management. You might be wise to start out with the attitude that everything is teasing rather than testing. Then, if it doesn't last long, you have automatically solved the problem.

But if the teasing continues for a long period of time, you will know that it is personal testing and that it is probably the product of genuine hostility. When this happens, you have a real challenge ahead of you. For example, one of your fellow employees may refuse to accept you. He may harass you at every turn. He may not give you a chance to be a normal, productive employee. The needle will be out at every opportunity.

Ray had this kind of experience when he was assigned to a maintenance crew with a gas and water company. The job was extremely important to him because it had taken him a long time to get it. He also knew that he was on a very strict ninety-day probation period. Because of this, Ray decided that he would go all out to keep his personal productivity high and still build good relationships with the rest of the crew.

Everything would have been great if it had not been for Art, who started out the very first day using every technique in the book to slow Ray down and get under his skin. Art constantly came up with comments like: "What are you trying to do, Ray, make us all look bad?" "Who are you kissin' up to by working so hard?" "If you slow down a little, kid, we'll get you through probation."

After three weeks of this Ray knew he was up against a personality conflict loaded with hostility. Rather than take it any longer, he invited Art to have coffee with him after work one day. It was a strained evening, but Art finally relaxed. Much of the hostility disappeared, and the next day he was off Ray's back. Ray never discovered the real cause of the conflict. The crew seemed happier, and productivity was better.

Chances are good that it will never happen to you personally, but occasionally an employee will get on the receiving end of some nonorganizational or personal testing from a supervisor. This is what happened to both Rachel and Jess.

Rachel, a young black woman, graduated near the top of her class in nursing school. She took the first job she interviewed for as a vocational nurse in a large home for elderly people. But Rachel quickly discovered that she was on the receiving end of some rather vicious testing from her supervisor.

She was not surprised when she received a lot of ugly jobs her first few days. She knew it was traditional, so she pleasantly went about giving baths to some of the most difficult patients. She had many disagreeable duties, all of which were assigned to her by the supervisor, a registered nurse who had been at the home for many years.

Rachel didn't complain; she didn't want any special favors because she was black. She took everything that came her way because she wanted to prove to herself that she could take it. But slowly she began to sense there was something more than just routine testing involved. Her supervisor seemed to dish out the ugly assignments with a strange, subtle bitterness. Not only that, but even after two new vocational nurses had joined the staff, Rachel was still doing all the really dirty jobs.

Although she was fearful of racial prejudice from the beginning, she tried to play it cool and hope for a change. She said nothing. But soon her fellow workers, most of whom were her age and also vocational nurses, got the message. When they did, a confrontation took place that finally reached the desk of the owner. The pressure on Rachel was quickly removed, and no one was sorry a week later when the registered nurse responsible resigned.

It is sometimes impossible to know the deep-seated motives behind some of the serious testing that takes place. Often the people re-

sponsible do not know themselves. Racial prejudice is only one of
the many causes, as the case involving Jess will illustrate.

> Jess was really pleased about his new construction job. At last he
> would be able to put his apprenticeship training to work and make
> some good money. He anticipated all the teasing he got from the old-
> timers at the beginning, and he took it in stride without any big
> scenes. But his foreman's attitude was something else. No matter
> how hard he tried, Jess got the needle from his foreman at every
> turn. No matter how much work Jess turned out, the foreman was
> on his back.
>
> Jess took it for about a week, and then, in desperation, he asked
> the advice of one of the older crew members. Here is what the older
> man said: "Look, buddy, our beloved supervisor is an uptight con-
> servative. Your long hair, your flashy sports car, and especially your
> free and easy lifestyle all get to him. Frankly, I think he has some
> trouble with his own sons and you remind him of them. At any rate,
> he's all wrong. What you do to get him off your back, though, is
> your own problem. Good luck."
>
> Jess gave it some serious thought and decided that he would face
> the foreman and see what happened. It was a tough decision to make
> because he didn't want to lose his job. He waited until they could be
> alone, and then he put all his cards on the table. He said, "You've
> been on my back, and you know it. I think you should either tell me
> why or start treating me the way you treat the others." There were
> some tense and awkward moments, but when it was all over the fore-
> man managed a small smile, and from then on things were noticeably
> better for Jess.

These two examples represent only a few of the many different
cases that could be presented. Sometimes sexual harassment is
involved. Sometimes supervisors are responsible; sometimes they
are not. The question is, of course, what can you do if you come
up against a serious testing situation?

Here are a few pointers that may help you.

Accept the situation willingly until you have time to analyze it
carefully. Take it as part of the test period and conduct yourself
in such a manner as not to aggravate the situation. It may pass
by itself, or someone else, without your knowledge, may come to
your rescue. If time does not take care of it and you come to the
point where you sincerely feel that you are being pushed too far,
approach the person who is doing the needling with a "let's lay
all the cards on the table" attitude. In your own words, without
hostility, say something like this: "If I have done anything to
upset you, please tell me. Otherwise, I feel it is time we started
to respect each other."

This will not be easy for you to do. But in cases of extreme testing, it is necessary to make the tester account for his or her actions. There is no other answer.

Unfortunately, some individuals will push you around indefinitely if you permit it. And if you permit it, they will never respect you. Chances are that this will not happen to you, but if it does, you must stand up to the situation and solve it yourself. It is important to you and to the company that you do so.

Of course, you need to go about it in the right way. Try not to have a chip on your shoulder. Do not make accusations. Try not to say anything personal about the man or woman you are standing up to. Your goal is to open up the relationship, to find a foundation upon which you can build for the future. Your goal is to demolish the psychological barrier, not to find out who is responsible for it. You must make it easy for the other person to save face. In most cases of testing (even when a healthy relationship has yet to be built), the principles and techniques found in Chapter 10, "Restoring Injured Relationships," are applicable, and it may be helpful to consider them.

Unless the testing is extremely severe or prolonged, you may be better off not going to others either inside or outside your organization for help. You will be respected for taking care of the problem yourself. If, however, you have made every effort to clear it up over a reasonable length of time and you have had no success, you should go to your supervisor and discuss it honestly and freely. Situations of this kind should not be permitted to continue to the point where departmental morale and productivity are impaired.

If you can prove that discrimination or sexual harassment has been involved, you should feel free to take your case to your local Fair Practices Labor Board.

It is important not to anticipate such situations. They are very rare. Such a problem may never come your way. For the most part, teasing and testing will be good-natured—maybe even enjoyable—if you have the right attitude.

Problem 12

Confrontation

"A person's attitude can stand just so much."

Jane graduated from a state college as a home economics major. She was ambitious, talented, and determined. In practically no time she had a good position with a giant retail operation, working in a laboratory where all consumer products purchased by the buyers were tested for safety, wearability, and other standards.

Jane received many compliments on her work from her supervisor. In addition, she was able to build good relationships with all her co-workers — except Ms. Robertson. Ms. Robertson was a long-time employee of the company and very critical of Jane. She was constantly making unkind and seemingly uncalled-for remarks about Jane.

One day Jane decided to do something about it. By checking around, she discovered that two previous employees has resigned because of Ms. Robertson. This made Jane feel that there was nothing personal about the trouble she was having. With this in mind, she waited for the right opportunity to meet Ms. Robertson alone, and this is what she said:

"Ms. Robertson, I have been here for two months and I seem to be getting along with everyone but you. I like my job. I want to keep it. If I have done anything to offend you, please tell me and I'll certainly make a change. I want very much to win your respect, but I do not intend to put up with your unfair treatment of me any longer."

Did Jane do the right thing? Was she too forceful in her approach? What would you have done in her place? If you were the supervisor, how would you resolve the conflict? (For a suggested answer, see page 192.)

CHAPTER 13

"What? Late again?"

ABSENTEEISM AND HUMAN RELATIONS

"Sorry I didn't show up for work yesterday, Rich. I had a little too much to drink at Harry's party, so I decided to stay in the sack and sleep it off."

"Hope things weren't too hard on you last Friday, Alice. I had a case of the blahs, so I stayed home and got a few personal things taken care of."

"Did you hear that sick crack from my supervisor, Marge? She sure gets uptight when I'm a little late now and then. You'd think that I'd committed a major crime."

"Don't breathe a word to the boss, Linda, but I'm going to make this a three-day weekend so I can go on a hiking trip. See you Tuesday."

"I've got to sneak out and take care of something personal, Art. Cover for me while I'm gone, will you?"

Absenteeism is a phenomenon that management lives with on a daily basis. So is the problem of lateness and employees leaving their work stations without authorization. Most experts agree that fewer and fewer people are taking pride in their attendance or on-time records. Why?

Those close to the scene have come up with many answers. Here are four frequently cited: (1) people do not commit themselves to a career or company as much these days, so they do not feel as much pressure to live up to the rules; (2) schools and colleges are so relaxed that the adjustment to the discipline of business is more difficult than it was in the past; (3) many people no longer feel obligated to live up to attendance standards or rules imposed on them by organizations; and (4) people allow personal problems to spill over into their work environment more than in the past.

What is the basic policy that most business and government organizations have toward absenteeism and reporting to work late? What is acceptable and what is not? What is management's attitude toward the problem, and what action do they take with those who consistently violate their policies?

Most professional managers in business and government will endorse and try to get their employees to live within the framework and spirit of the following policy:

Employees should not come to work when one of the following conditions exist:

1. When it might endanger their own health or that of their co-workers

2. When the employee is in a psychological or emotional state that could hurt on-the-job productivity and possibly create an unsafe condition

3. When a serious personal or family emergency exists.

If none of the above conditions exists, employees should be on the job and, except in special cases, they should be there on time.

This policy might sound harsh and autocratic, but organizations have had years of experience with the problem and they feel that, unless they take a firm stand, they will be misinterpreted by some and taken advantage of by others. Here are their reasons for following such a policy.

In order to make a profit and stay in business, most organizations must operate under tight production and service schedules. These schedules are built around employees. An assembly line from which a few workers are absent is no longer an assembly line. When a customer wants to buy something in a retail store and there is nobody available to help him, a sale can be lost. A customer goes to a restaurant and if his waitress is doing the work of two because another waitress didn't show up, the customer may never return.

Management has learned that when an employee or supervisor doesn't show up for work as scheduled, immediate and costly adjustments are necessary if production is to continue and customers are to be kept happy. Sometimes, but not always, the other employees can pitch in and fill the gap. But most of the time, the company pays at least a small price in loss of efficiency, loss of sales, or loss of customer faith. In short, the absence of an employee usually costs the company money in one way or another. If the absence is necessary, nobody complains. But if the absence is unnecessary, then management must become concerned and involved.

Chronic lateness by an employee, although not usually as serious or expensive for the company as absenteeism, is still a problem. A late employee can delay the changing of shifts. An employee who is constantly late can emotionally upset a conscientious supervisor and make her (or him) more difficult for others to work with for the rest of the day. Most serious of all is the negative influence the consistently late employee has on the productivity of others. The supervisor who takes a soft approach to such an employee stands the chance of losing the respect of other, more reliable employees.

But absenteeism, lateness, and unauthorized time away from work are not only management problems. They should also be viewed as problems and challenges to the employee himself (or herself). That is primarily what this chapter is about. How should *you* look at these problems? How will they influence *your* future?

Supervisors and workers alike who fail to build a good record in these areas will almost always pay a very high price as far as their relationships with others are concerned. Here is why.

1. *A poor attendance record will keep you from building good horizontal working relationships with your co-workers. They may deeply resent having to carry an extra load when you are absent.* Few kinds of behavior will destroy a relationship more than being frequently absent and causing co-workers to "carry" you in your own department.

2. *A poor record will strain the vertical working relationship with your supervisor. It will make more work for her (or him) personally, it will cause her department to be less efficient, and it will put her on the spot with other employees.* Most experts agree that it is almost impossible for an employee who is guilty of chronic absenteeism to maintain a healthy relationship with an immediate supervisor.

In addition to the preceding two basic reasons, the following four should receive consideration.

1. Excessive absenteeism and lateness will build a credibility gap between you and management. This can seriously hurt your future because those who cannot be depended upon are seldom promoted. It should also be pointed out that, right or wrong, some management people feel there is a moral aspect to the problem. If an individual accepts employment, he or she agrees to abide by the rules, within reason. Absence without sufficient cause is interpreted by management people as moral failure.

2. Records that reflect heavy absenteeism and lateness are permanent and can be forwarded upon request to other organizations. The record you are building now could help or hurt you, should you decide to move elsewhere.

3. If you have a good record, a request to be absent for personal and nonemergency reasons will seem more acceptable.

4. In case of layoffs, cutbacks, and reassignments, those people with poor records are usually the first to be terminated or reassigned.

Most organizations want to be understanding about employees' problems. They realize that there are exceptions to the rules, and they are willing to listen and make adjustments. Employees who consistently abuse the rules are usually counseled and given adequate warning. Those who play it straight with their companies usually receive fair and just treatment in return. To illustrate the causes and results of absenteeism and lateness among employees and supervisors, the following five examples are cited.

Dennis was a productive worker. When he was on the job and feeling well, nobody could complain about him. He had plenty of skill, a great sense of humor, and he was always willing to pitch in and help others. His only real problem was drinking. Every other week he would really tie one on and call in sick.

About a year ago Dennis and his supervisor had a series of heart-to-heart talks about Dennis's drinking. Three months later Dennis and a counselor from the Human Resource Department discussed the problem on three different occasions. Six months ago — half a year since his first talk with the supervisor — Dennis was referred to the company physician for professional help. Last week, with full documentation by the organization, Dennis was reluctantly given his termination notice. His record showed that he had been absent over thirty days the previous year. The organization Dennis worked for had tried to help, but Dennis had refused to help himself.

When she first came to work, Judy showed great promise. She had all the skills necessary to become a top-flight employee, and she was great with people. Among some of the staff, she quickly became known as the "too" girl. She was too pretty, too vivacious, and too popular. She also received too many invitations to too many parties, and as a result, she was absent too frequently.

It became clear to her supervisor that Judy just didn't have the physical endurance to lead such an active social life and hold down a demanding full-time job at the same time. During the first six months of employment, she was absent eleven times, each time for one day, and her excuse was always illness. After repeated counseling, Judy's supervisor finally asked that she be transferred to another department. Management made an attempt to do this, but when other supervisors checked on her absentee record, they refused to accept her. After additional, unsuccessful counseling, management had to let her go.

Katherine was highly ambitious, talented, energetic, and respected by both fellow employees and management. Everybody expected her to move a long way up the executive ladder. She seemed programmed for success. But Katherine's desire for quick recognition and more money caused her to hurt her reputation inside the company. Here is the story.

Katherine took a moonlighting job with a musical group that was good enough to get four or five bookings each week. The job paid good money, but it demanded a great deal of energy. After a few months, Katherine not only looked beat, but her on-the-job productivity started to drop. Soon she started calling in sick from time to time. Within six months she had seriously hurt her reputation.

Fortunately for Katherine, she had an understanding supervisor. After some counseling, Katherine quit her moonlighting and started to build back the fine reputation she had once enjoyed. It cost her at least one promotion, but Katherine did learn one lesson: any outside activity that drains one's energy to the point where frequent absences are necessary eventually spells trouble.

Vicki was an excellent salesperson in a fashion department. She was so good, in fact, that she was being trained as a fashion coordinator and buyer. But Vicki had one bad habit she simply could not shake. She simply could not organize her day to the point where she could get to work on time. Her timecard showed that she was from five to fifteen minutes late two or three times each week.

Vicki's supervisor and the store manager counseled her. Nobody wanted to lose her, but in the final analysis management had to weigh the influence of her lateness on the morale and productivity of others. When this was done, the decision to release Vicki was reluctantly made. She didn't have any trouble getting another job, but the new job didn't have the potential of the one she had lost, and the new management was less tolerant of her problem.

A national chain organization was forced to cut back its work force because of lower sales. It was decided that they could get by with one instead of two employees in a particular department in one of their stores. One individual would be transferred to a less desirable job in another section.

A careful analysis was made to see which of two people should be moved. Both were highly respected, and they were equal in all but two respects. One employee had three years' seniority over the other, so normally she would stay. But her absentee record was much poorer than the other employees'. Management decided that the employee with the better attendance record deserved to keep the better job. When the employee with seniority was notified and given the reason for the decision, she admitted she had no defense.

These cases are just a few examples of how employees can hurt their long-range careers by frequent absenteeism or chronic lateness. Here are a few tips that will help you:

1. Stay home under the following conditions: (a) when you are honestly sick and feel it would hurt your health or that of others if you reported to work, (b) when your emotional or mental condition is such that you know you could not contribute to the productivity of the department and might endanger the safety of others, and (c) when you have a family emergency and are urgently needed at home.

2. Notify the company at once of your decision to stay home. Tell them in an honest and straightforward way why you can't make it. Talk to your supervisor, not to a co-worker.

3. If you stay at home for more than a single day because of illness, it is wise to provide a daily progress report on your condition. Also estimate when you will be able to return.

4. Save your authorized sick-leave time for real emergencies. It is a cushion that might come in handy. If you never use it, you should assume the attitude that you were lucky you didn't have to.

5. Always give yourself a little lead time when getting ready to report to work. Do not put yourself in a position where a small

delay will make you late. It is better to be ten minutes early than one minute late. On those rare occasions when you are late, give management a real reason for it.

6. Take your allotted breaks, but don't be absent from your work station longer than the specified time. People who always stretch their coffee breaks are not appreciated by their co-workers or supervisor. When emergencies do come up and you must forgo or delay a scheduled break, don't nurse a feeling that you have been cheated and that you need an extra-long break to make up for it.

7. Don't be absent from your work station for long, unless you work it out in advance with your supervisor. Also, let your co-workers and/or your supervisor know where you will be when you are away. The best way to keep a supervisor from breathing down your neck is to earn your freedom by keeping him (or her) adequately informed.

8. When you have a special reason for being absent from work, such as a family wedding, funerals, or court appearances, work it out as far in advance as possible with your supervisor.

A good record shows management that you are sensitive to the needs of others. It shows them that you are a motivated, rather than reluctant worker. It shows them that you are ready for better opportunities.

Problem 13

Balance

"Nobody could balance my act."

It is easy to like Lorraine. She is highly efficient at her job, always willing to pitch in to help others, and often forgoes her break or stays late to catch up on her work. There is only one major problem: excessive absenteeism. Some of Lorraine's co-workers often bet on just which day of the week she will fail to show.

The problem lies in Lorraine's inability to balance home and career. A single parent (a highly protective mother of a three-year-old girl called Sissy), Lorraine sometimes stays home to catch up on home chores, change babysitters, or when Sissy has the sniffles. When Lorraine calls in (she doesn't always do this), her excuse almost always relates to an illness — either her own or Sissy's.

Over the last three months departmental productivity has dropped measurably because of adjustments made to compensate for Lorraine's absences. Her relationships with her supervisor and co-workers are paper thin.

How far, in your opinion, should Lorraine's supervisor and company go to protect her job? (For a suggested answer, see page 193.)

"Mistakes? Don't look at me!"

CHAPTER **14**

FIVE COMMON HUMAN-RELATIONS MISTAKES

Both new and experienced employees make human-relations mistakes that damage their personal progress. It is the purpose of this chapter to single out and fully explain the implications of five of the most common mistakes:

1. Failure to listen

2. Underestimating others

3. Failure to report or admit mistakes to management

4. Failure to provide your own motivation

5. Permitting others to turn you into a victim

Failure to Listen

The art of listening is a basic human-relations skill. Many excellent books have been written on the subject. Your public library should contain several of these books. If you read just one you will improve your competency in this area. Our discussion of the art of listening will be brief and to the point.

The first step in learning how to listen is to learn how to concentrate. Hearing is a selective process. Most people hear only what they want to hear. Your problem, then, is to listen to what is important and push other sounds to the outer edge of your hearing. There are so many sounds around you that you may not be picking up the ones that are vital to your happiness and success.

On the job, hearing is a matter of practical communication. When a supervisor or fellow worker wishes to transmit an idea, a warning, or a change in procedure to you, he (or she) usually does it verbally. There may be other sounds he cannot eliminate. It may be the end of the day, and you may be tired. His words may mean one thing to him and another to you. Good, clear, accurate communication is never easy.

Let us assume, however, that the person initiating the message does the best job possible. Does this ensure that you will receive the message? Of course not! You are the receiver, and if your mind is focused elsewhere when the message is transmitted, *you may hear the sounds but fail to get the message.*

Advertising executives and specialists have recognized for years how difficult it is to get a verbal message home. This difficulty is most apparent in television commercials. There, the name of the product is often repeated six times in thirty seconds. If you are really listening, you might feel that such repetition is an insult to your ability to receive. You would be justified in this reaction. But the advertising people do not assume that you are a good listener. They assume that you are a typical (that is, poor) listener. Consequently, to be sure the product name makes an impression, they pound it home through repetition.

Your supervisor is not an advertising expert, nor does she (or he) have the time to pound her message home. She feels she should be able to say it once and have it understood. She assumes you are a good listener.

Sometimes it is very difficult just to sit back and listen. There are three basic reasons why this is true. First, people are often so busy with their own thoughts and desires, related and nonrelated, that they are 90 percent sender and only 10 percent receiver. When this happens, the communication system breaks down. Second, some individuals are self-centered. Instead of listening to what is being said, they are merely waiting for the speaker to finish so that they can talk. Getting their thoughts organized keeps them from being good listeners. Third, some people allow themselves to analyze motives or personality traits of the person speaking and, again, fail to hear what is being said.

In business and industry, the ability to listen is often a matter of dollars and cents. A draftsman who doesn't hear an architect tell him to make a certain change in a blueprint can cause the loss of thousands of dollars when a bid is accepted on specifications that are not correct. A salesperson who fails to hear a message from a client, and as a result does not comply with an important delivery date, can lose not only the sale, but also a valued customer.

Communications problems can also cost money inside factories. For example, Daniel's failure to receive and retain the right message from his shop foreman cost his company a considerable amount of money. Here is the story.

> On his way to his regular morning coffee break, and somewhat preoccupied with his own thoughts, Dan was stopped by his foreman and told to change the tolerance on a machine part he would be turning out for the rest of that day. After his coffee break, Dan returned to his machine, made an adjustment, and worked hard the rest of the day to complete all of the parts. The following day he was called on the carpet for producing parts that were too small. What had happened? Dan had been told to *increase* the size of the part, but he had *decreased* it instead. His failure to receive—and retain—the right message was a serious mistake, and it cost his company money in terms of both time and materials.

You can think of many other examples. It can even be said that when safety precautions are the subject of the message, the ability to listen can be a matter of life and death.

Let's look at your ability to listen from the viewpoint of your supervisor, who is, after all, the primary sender of important messages to you. Here are four questions you can ask yourself to determine whether you are a good listener:

1. Does your supervisor have to fight to get your attention?

2. Do you find yourself thinking about something else the moment your supervisor starts talking?

3. Does your supervisor insult you by repeating the message because he senses you are a poor listener? Or do you find you must go back and ask him to repeat it?

4. Do you sometimes feel confused about instructions given to you when you start to do the job requested?

If you can say no to these questions, you may be a good listener. If not, you should concentrate on improving. The following tips should help you.

1. Always look at the person who is sending the message; this will help you to concentrate and close out unimportant noises.

2. If your supervisor has trouble sending out clear signals, you must make the extra effort to listen more carefully. Although it is primarily his or her responsibility to be a good sender, it is still to your advantage to receive the message as clearly as possible.

3. So that you will remember the message, jot it down in your notebook. Repeat it in your own mind a few times. Put any change ordered in the message into practice as soon as possible. When appropriate, repeat the message to your supervisor.

4. Refrain from coming up with an excuse when you receive criticism. You will improve more if you listen to what you are doing wrong rather than quickly coming to your own defense.

5. Think, reply briefly if necessary, and then continue to listen, so that you receive the complete message.

6. Always ask questions right away if you don't understand something. If you don't do this, you may not fully get the message that follows.

7. If you find yourself in conversation with someone who is overly talkative, do not hesitate to interrupt after a polite period of time. If you do not do this, you may become so irritated you may not listen anyway.

Being a good listener is not easy. It will take a conscientious effort on your part. But one of the finest compliments you will ever receive from a superior will be something like this: "One thing I really like about Harry is that if you tell him something once, you know he's got it. You never have to tell him twice."

Underestimating Others

The second of the five big mistakes, according to Human Resources people, is that of underestimating others.

A superior or co-worker may not appear to be doing much from your limited perspective. You might, therefore, wrongly assume that he or she is coasting. This could be a big mistake.

Here is a simple case to emphasize the point.

Henry accepted a job with a major metropolitan department store. After thirty days of training, he was temporarily assigned to work with Ms. Smith, the manager of inexpensive women's apparel.

Henry soon discovered that he was part of a rather hectic operation. Merchandise moved in and out of the department quickly. Ms. Smith was not an impressive person to Henry. Her desk was disorderly. She seem to move in many directions at the same time. She seemed to spend more time than necessary talking to the employees.

Henry decided that he had drawn an unfortunate first assignment.

It was his good luck, to meet a young buyer at lunch one day. From this women he learned that Ms. Smith had the most profitable department in the store and an outstanding reputation with all top management people. Ms. Smith had trained more of the store's executives than any other person. It was then obvious that Henry had received one of the best assignments and had seriously underestimated Ms. Smith.

The new employee in this case learned a big lesson without getting hurt. He quickly changed his attitude toward his supervisor before the relationship was seriously damaged. He was fortunate.

When you fail to build a quality relationship with a supervisor or co-worker because you underestimate. them, you may hurt yourself in the following ways. Your negative attitude may cause you to learn less from this person than you otherwise would. Coworkers may sense the mistake you are making and see your attitude as a sign of immaturity. The individual you have misjudged may pick up your attitude and resent it, causing a serious human-relations problem.

If you are a new employee or have recently accepted a new assignment, remind yourself that you are in the poorest position to estimate the power, influence, and contribution that others are making to the organization, *especially when these people are already in management positions.* You will be smart to avoid prejudging others. Different people make different contributions to the growth and profit of an organization. Top management can see this, but you usually cannot.

If the temptation is too great, and you must at times question the effectiveness of others, keep your impressions to yourself. You can easily trap yourself by being a Monday-morning quarterback. Underestimating the value of others can keep you from building relationships that are important to your personal progress.

Failure to Report or Admit Mistakes to Management

A third common human-relations mistake is failure to admit or report to management personal errors in judgment or violations of company procedures, rules, and regulations.

Everyone makes minor blunders from time to time. Even a good employee is not perfect. Precise and methodical people sometimes make mistakes in calculations. Logical thinkers who pride themselves on their scientific approach to decision making will sometimes make an error in judgment. A conscientious person who is very loyal to his organization will, on occasion, violate a company rule or regulation before he knows it.

These things happen to the best of people, and unless you are a most unusual person they will happen to you. These little mistakes will not damage your career if you admit them openly. They can, however, cause considerable damage if you try to cover them up and in so doing compound the original mistake. To illustrate, let us take the incident of the dented fender.

> Ken worked for a large banking organization. One of his numerous responsibilities was to deliver documents to various branch operations in the banking system. To do this, he would check out a company car from the transportation department.
>
> On one such assignment, Ken dented the fender of a company car while backing out of a crowded parking lot. He knew that he should report the damage to the dispatcher, but the dent was so insignificant he thought it would go unnoticed. Why make a federal case out of a little scratch? Why spoil a clean record with the company over something so unimportant.
>
> Two days later Ken was called into the private office of his department manager. It was an embarrassing twenty minutes. He had to admit that he was responsible for the damage and that he had broken a company rule by not reporting it. The incident was then closed.
>
> The slight damage to the company car was a human error anyone could make. The big mistake Ken made was in not reporting it. Looking back on the incident, he admitted that the damage to the car was far less than the damage to his relationships with others.

Most little mistakes, and sometimes many big mistakes, are accepted and forgotten when they are openly and quickly reported. Throwing up a smoke screen to cover them is asking for trouble. The second mistake may be more damaging than the first.

Failure to Provide Your Own Motivation

The modern approach by management to provide the best possible working environment — *and then give employees the freedom to motivate themselves in their own way* — often leaves a few individuals on the sidelines unmotivated. It is a human-relations mistake to allow yourself to fall into this category.

New employees are expected to possess sufficient self-confidence to engage themselves in the normal work process without always having to be nudged by others; experienced workers are expected to stay alert and productive without special counseling by their supervisors. Those who stand or sit around while co-workers are busily involved in productivity set themselves apart, and, in so doing, injure their relationships with both supervisors and fellow employees.

In the workplace everyone is expected to be a part of the "work team" and contribute at acceptable norms. Those who wait around expecting or refusing to be motivated leave themselves on the sidelines where learning opportunities and promotional possibilities are limited.

Of course, anyone can occasionally have an "off day." But self-motivation is primarily an attitude of consistent willingness to do whatever it takes (within legal and ethical bounds) to get the job done, while meeting established timeliness and quality standards. Initially, it may take some extra effort to get your internal (self-motivation) generator going. Be willing to try harder and go the "extra mile" for your organization without constant prodding. More than likely, your managers will be more willing to reciprocate.

Permitting Others to Turn You into a Victim

When people are unfortunate and become victims of automobile accidents or needless crimes, they often pay a high price. The consequences can be similarly serious when we become human-relations victims. Consider the following:

- Statistically only a small percentage of people become direct victims of serious crime. Everyone eventually becomes a victim of a damaged relationship.

- Financial loss due to robbery, fraud, or physical injury can be high. So can the loss of career opportunity that results from unrepaired relationships.

- The emotional and psychological damage of being a human-relations victim can sometimes be as traumatic as being a victim of crime. Becoming a victim of a damaged relationship can cause moodiness, loss of confidence, resentfulness, indignation, and mental distress.

There are three primary ways people needlessly victimize themselves:

1. When they refuse to correct human-relations mistakes quickly.

2. When they do not make an effort to correct a "no-fault" situation.

3. When they permit the emotionalism of a relationship conflict to chew them up inside.

Many times a conflict will emerge within a relationship and both parties become increasingly involved in a process that accelerates to more damaging stages.

Stage 1: Only surface damage. Low "hurt" involvement. Restoration possibilities excellent. No harm, no foul.
Stage 2: Emotional damage usually more serious for one individual than the other. Restoration more difficult.
Stage 3: As a result of lack of communication, conflict becomes needlessly severe. Both parties become victims. Professional counseling may be needed.

The process will vary depending on the individuals and the nature of the conflict. Once started, however, it often becomes a continuous development, until both parties become "losers." Thus, the sooner any damage—no matter how slight—is repaired, the better. Just as both individuals can become victims, both can also become winners.

To help the reader avoid self-victimization, the following suggestions are made.

- Read Chapter 9 a second time, to learn how to release your aggressions harmlessly.

- Remember that the more meaningful a relationship is to you, the higher the risk of self-victimization, should a conflict occur.

- A substitute phrase for self-victimization is "holding a grudge."

- Let small irritations pass.

- Every time a relationship conflict occurs, ask yourself this question: *Who will become the ultimate victim?*

Obviously as you become more competent at human relations, fewer conflicts will surface and there is less of a chance you will become a victim. But once a conflict develops, you become vulnerable and the steps you take to restore the relationship are critical. If you are not willing to take action (regardless of who may be at fault), you may nullify much of the human-relations progress you have made.

Problem 14

Motivation

"Berry's O.K. — he
just needs motivation."

Berry graduated near the top of his class academically. In addition, he is excellent at balancing his many technical skills with human-relations competencies. With all of his advantages, one would expect Berry to be highly successful in his first career position. Not so. After six months Berry's boss called him into his office and said: "Berry, you've got everything going for you; but for some reason, you expect others to motivate you. As a result, you are out of step with your co-workers. Frankly, I don't have the time or patience to motivate you through long-term counseling. Even if I did, I wouldn't know where to start. Unless you are willing to try motivating yourself, it won't happen around here, and you will be the loser."

What, in your opinion, is wrong? What can Berry do to become a self-motivated professional? (For a suggested answer, see page 194.)

"You call that ethical?"

CHAPTER 15

BUSINESS ETHICS, RUMORS, AND THE CONFIDENCE TRIANGLE

Dr. Albert Schweitzer once said: "In a general sense, ethics is the name we give to our concern for good behavior. We feel an obligation to consider not only our own well-being but also that of others and human society as a whole."

Business ethics involves being fully aware of what we are doing in the area of human relationships. Are we treating people the way they want to be treated? Are we complying with rules, such as the laws of the land, the customs and expectations of the community, the principles of morality, and the policies of the organization? Are we being true to ourselves?

Honesty, truthfulness, loyalty, and respect have relevance in the work environment, but "gray areas" exist:

- An honest employee who would never steal money from a cash box might use the company car to run personal errands while making sales rounds.

- A high-producing, devoted employee might work overtime in an emergency, but tell his boss he got caught in traffic upon arriving late the next day when, in fact, he overslept.

- A sympathetic employee knows a co-worker is operating a

134

small business on the side (often using company office equipment and paper) but says nothing.

Obviously, maintaining high ethical standards is not easy when co-workers may view the subject differently. Here are three attitudes that can help you throw off temptations and be true to yourself.

Respect company rules, procedures, and standards. Remember, you can be unethical without breaking the law. Use common sense and assess the potential damage of an unethical act to your career. Violations are not worth it in the long run.

Be willing to test your ethical thinking frequently. Ask yourself: "Is this the right thing to do? Is it fair? Is it honest? Am I creating a guilt feeling for nothing?"

Keep reminding yourself that relationships are built upon trust. Unethical behavior can destroy relationships because it is difficult to respect an individual who flirts with accepted ethical standards.

Here are seven mistakes to avoid.

1. Misrepresenting the facts about my job activities or those of a co-worker.

2. Divulging personal or confidential information to co-workers, customers, competitors, or the general public.

3. Permitting, or failing to report, violations of any federal, state, or municipal laws or regulations.

4. Protecting unethical co-workers from corrective discipline.

5. Condoning or failing to report the theft or misuse of company property.

6. Covering up on-the-job accidents and failing to report health and safety hazards.

7. Passing on co-workers' ideas as your own.

Rumors

Webster's New World Dictionary gives us this definition of *rumor:* "General talk not based on definite knowledge; mere gossip; hearsay; an unconfirmed report, story, or statement in general circulation."

All organizations have information collectors—employees who set up and maintain informal networks that keep them informed about what is going on at all times. This is generally a harmless activity, providing it doesn't interfere with the employee's personal productivity and is not used to spread rumors and malicious gossip.

Unauthenticated reports, or rumors, seem to originate and circulate within every group of people, especially when a group's members have common interests and competitive goals. Rumors are common in small communities, social and service groups, schools, churches, and, of course, business organizations.

Rumors are based on people's need to share their anxieties with others. Some rumors get started because of faulty communication or unintentional misinterpretation of the original message. Others are in the form of malicious gossip designed to hurt another person.

Two popular expressions have become associated with the circulation of rumors. One is *rumor mill*. This familiar expression implies that rumors, like grain begin processed in a mill, are turned out regularly in large numbers, altered, and circulated within the confines of a certain group or organization. Workers who are information collectors are all too frequently the chief providers of grist for the rumor mills.

The second popular expression is *grapevine*, which means an unofficial, confidential, person-to-person chain of verbal communication. The grapevine can best be viewed as an underground network that operates within an organization. The rumor mill may get the message started, but the grapevine keeps it moving. The grapevine has the reputation of operating without official sanction, and usually the information transmitted has an aura of secrecy.

Not all information that gets into the rumor mill and travels along the grapevine is false. It can be the truth. But the person who introduces the information must have the facts right, and those facts must be transmitted without misinterpretation. These conditions are, of course, seldom present. Even when the original information is accurate, facts can become distorted as they move along the grapevine.

The important thing to realize is that information processed through the rumor mill and passed along the grapevine is not reliable. It may not be based upon the facts. It may be slanted to serve the interests of a second, third, or fourth party. It may even be malicious.

For these reasons the rumor mill should be viewed with considerable caution, and information coming through the grapevine should be discounted. You cannot depend on it.

Because rumors occur in all organizations, it is only natural to find them in business and industrial concerns. It follows that there may be a rumor mill in your organization. If there is, be forewarned. Accepting rumors as the truth can cause you to make serious human-relations mistakes. You might, for example damage a good horizontal or vertical relationship you have built; or you might permit false information to get in the way of building a relationship that would contribute to higher productivity, and perhaps, enhance your own progress.

What is management's position in this matter? This book, of course, cannot speak for your particular management. However, this much can be said: the term *rumor mill* is not new to those in leadership positions, and management usually knows when a grapevine exists.

This does not mean that the people responsible for management condone the grapevine, but they know when it is in operation. We know this because they occasionally step in and squelch a false rumor before damage is done to either an individual or the company. They might also deliberately leak some positive information into the grapevine so that employees will get an accurate message in a hurry.

You should realize that keeping employees fully informed on company matters through regular channels is a huge task. Conferences, bulletins, company periodicals, and other media are often not fully effective. But even if they were, it is doubtful that rumors would be eliminated. Management knows this. So if you are on the receiving end of rumors in your job, and you sense the existence of a rumor mill, this does not mean that management is not concerned. It is!

Management is aware that unfounded rumors can cause unnecessary anxiety among employees and that such anxiety hurts the morale of the organization. They know that rumors can sometimes be malicious and that innocent employees can be hurt. They will do what they can to prevent this.

In order to be successful, however, they need the help and support of every employee.

What might you do to help management? And, more important, what might you do to help yourself? Here are six suggestions.

1. The first thing is to admit that there is such a phenomenon as a rumor mill in your organization. If you are blind to this situation, you may introduce and transmit harmful rumors to others without knowing it.

2. All information received through the grapevine, especially if it has implications of intrigue, should be viewed with skepticism, and you should not permit this information to disturb you personally. If it is true, you will have time to adjust to it after you receive it from official sources. Be patient until you get the facts. Partial information is dangerous. Give management time to give you all the facts. Do not take any action or make decisions until you know.

3. Do not be guilty yourself of introducing rumors into the grapevine. You may, by accident, overhear something of a confidential nature and pass it on to someone as the truth, only to discover at a later date that you only heard part of the story. Or you may see something a little unusual and draw the wrong conclusion, as in the following case.

> Rebecca noticed her supervisor, a young married man, taking her coworker, Florence, who was divorced, home two nights in succession. She decided there was something going on between them and introduced the matter into the local grapevine. As so often happens, the rumor got out of hand. A number of people, including Rebecca herself, got hurt. The supervisor was transferred and his replacement was less effective. What was the truth? Florence had put her car in the repair shop for two days, and the supervisor had volunteered to take her home so that she would not have to walk the dark streets alone. Nothing more was involved.

4. Refuse to pass unsubstantiated information you receive secondhand. If you do this, you may break the circuit in the grapevine and perhaps keep others from being disturbed unnecessarily. Sometimes, during coffee-break talks for instance, it may be possible to steer conversation away from rumors and onto harmless tracks, such as sports or TV shows.

5. If you must complain about company matters or company

people, do so in the proper manner to your immediate super-visor, or blow off steam at home or with a trusted person — but not with your fellow workers. This will eliminate the possibility of having your personal gripes misinterpreted and introduced into the rumor mill. It will also keep anyone from using your complaints to hurt your relationship with your superiors.

6. Try not to let a nonpersonal rumor that might involve your future with the company upset you until you get the facts. If you do, there might be a noticeable drop in your personal productiv-ity that will needlessly hurt your future. Make every effort to ig-nore a rumor until you receive official information. If you find you cannot do this, consult your supervisor or someone else in management for the facts before you draw unwarranted conclu-sions. Many employees have injured their future by premature action based upon a false rumor. Don't fall into this trap.

We could fill pages discussing the various kinds of rumors that travel along the grapevine. We could give many examples. It will serve our purpose best, however, to place them all into the fol-lowing two broad classifications.

Many on-the-job rumors involve people's personal lives and are not related to job situations. Some of these fall into the back-fence category. Some are little more than coffee-break gossip. Al-though there is considerable intrigue in such rumors, the new employee would be wise to keep working relationships strictly that and stay a safe distance from such rumors.

Rumors of the second kind concern the *organization*. They pertain to things that may or may not happen to the company. Although they influence employees, they are not personal. For example, there have been rumors about layoffs, with no founda-tion in fact; rumors that departments were to be eliminated when in fact they were to be enlarged; rumors of resignations when in fact none were ever contemplated; and rumors of termi-nations that turned out to be transfers.

Organizational rumors have an enormous influence on the pro-ductivity of employees and the general progress of the company. Management, by keeping the official channels of communication open, tries to eliminate them. Rumors continue to exist in most companies, however. Unless the employee develops a way to insulate himself (or herself) against them, he can become constantly insecure about his job and his future. His personal productivity will go up and down based upon the latest rumor. And all for nothing!

Confidence Triangle

Let's now look closely at one aspect of the problem from a positive point of view. Have you ever heard the expression *confidence triangle*? A confidence triangle is the way a confidential comment can be transmitted to a third party. The diagram below will help explain the idea.

We will assume you are Mr. A. You have a strong, healthy relationship with Mr. B. Occasionally you talk things over with him in confidence. One day at lunch you mention that Mr. C has been of great help to you in completing a certain project and that you have considerable respect for his ability and perception.

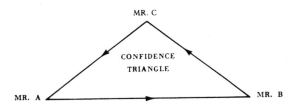

You do not realize, when you say this, that Mr. C has a strong, healthy relationship with Mr. B and that your comments will be transmitted to him. Of course, this will not hurt your relationship with Mr. C. In fact, it will improve it, because the favorable comments have been made in confidence and transmitted by a person Mr. C respects.

So far, the confidence triangle has worked in a positive manner. *But what if your comments had been negative?* Instead of improving your relationships with Mr. B and Mr. C, you would have damaged them. The confidence triangle works both ways. The truth is, then, that you can strengthen or weaken relationships with some people through others. When you say something positive about a third person to an individual with whom you have a good rapport, relationships can improve. When you say something negative, the opposite can happen.

Nobody likes to accept advice. Even when advice comes at the right time from the right person in the right way, it is difficult to accept. Yet, sometimes accepting advice is the smart thing to do.

Let us assume that at this very moment the conditions are ideal and you are willing to accept advice. What might be the best human-relations advice you could receive? In all probability it would be this:

If you can't say something good about a person, don't say anything at all.

Like most advice that comes in such simple terms, this precept is far easier to put into print than to put into practice. Yet the degree to which you observe this simple rule on your new job will have considerable influence on your success.

Understanding the nature of rumors, the power of the rumor mill, the scope of the grapevine, and the impact of the confidence triangle should teach you to be very careful about what you say to others.

It has been said that many human-relations problems are self-created. There is truth in this statement.

Problem 15

Dilemma

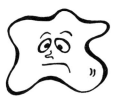

"Me? Fall for a rumor?"

Sylvia was young, serious-minded, well educated, and capable. More than anything else she wanted a management role with her company.

Sylvia worked hard for three years. She did an excellent job in human relations. Her personal productivity was never questioned. Ms. Smith, her supervisor, encouraged her to prepare to take over her job. She helped Sylvia a great deal in this respect, but, of course, she could make no promises.

About this time, Sylvia spent the evening with Helen, an intimate friend of hers. At one point Helen told Sylvia she had heard that a Mr. Young, an employee from another department, was being trained to take Ms. Smith's place as department head.

Although she said nothing and did not show it on the outside, Sylvia was very disturbed by the news. It was hard to believe that management could make such a decision so far in advance. She fretted about it constantly and could not keep her mind on her work. As a result, she made more and more mistakes, and certain important reports were turned in late. Over the next six months, the excellent relationship she had with her supervisor slowly deteriorated.

Then, just as Helen had said, Ms. Smith was promoted and Mr. Young was made department head in an official announcement from top management. Sylvia was deeply hurt and disappointed.

What mistakes did Sylvia make that might have contributed to her ultimate disappointment? (For a suggested answer, see page 194.)

CHAPTER **16**

"I hate decision making."

TWO ROUTES TO THE TOP

There are two basic paths to a top management position. One is to join and stay with a large organization, climbing the ladder of success rung by rung. The other is to move from one company to another, improving your position with each move. Those who prefer to move up within the same organization are *stabilizers*. Those who prefer the zigzag route are *scramblers*.

If you go about it in the right way, you can usually build a rich and rewarding career as a stabilizer. The practice that makes this possibility attractive is called *promotion from within*, or PFW.

There is nothing new about PFW. It has always been the custom to move those who demonstrate that they are capable and responsible into higher positions when vacancies occur. If effective people are available, management usually wants to promote from within the company's own ranks. This policy encourages loyalty, provides security, and has other advantages. It should be remembered, however, that even companies that have such a policy may make exceptions on their own or can be forced into adjustments because of layoffs and reorganizations.

In order to understand the implications of the PFW idea in a given corporation, one must study the organizational structure. Each company has grown to maturity in a different way — each firm has developed a different "culture." Every company has its own interpretation and application of a PFW policy.

Because of this, generalizations are dangerous. The reader must interpret the following pages in the light of the policies and practices of his or her own company. It is important, however, to give the new worker a perspective on his or her career possibilities. The triangle shown will get us started.

TOP MANAGEMENT

MIDDLE MANAGEMENT

JUNIOR MANAGEMENT

SUPERVISORY POSITIONS

PERSONNEL

This diagram could represent a business or an industrial or governmental organization. Size is not important. It could be a company with 200,000 employees or one with 200. Management—those people who are responsible for the leadership and direction of the company—is of course at the apex of the triangle. Some organizations divide management into four classifications: top management, middle management, junior management, and supervisory positions.

Top-management executives with giant concerns are usually the president and vice-presidents. Middle-management people are usually division heads and branch and plant managers. Junior management includes middle-management assistants, those whose positions fall just beneath the middle-management classification. Next in line come the many supervisors.

Below the management level are many kinds of personnel, depending on the type of organization. In a manufacturing business we find different levels of technical people: engineers, technicians, skilled craftsmen, semiskilled workers, and helpers. In other kinds of organizations, there are different patterns and different backgrounds.

Supervisory positions, as illustrated here, can outnumber higher-management positions. There is usually a supervisory position for every twelve employees in an organization; in some companies the ratio is lower. The supervisory position is extremely important to the new worker, for in most cases this is the first position leading to upper management.

Now that we have seen the top of the triangle, let us look at the bottom. All organizations employ the majority of new workers at lower-level entry positions.

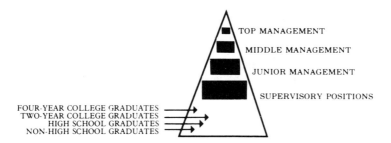

Not all companies have four entry levels. Some have only two or three. The important thing is that all employees have an opportunity to grow. Each employee, regardless of where he or she starts, can and should move upward in the organization. This is the meaning of PFW.

There are both advantages and disadvantages to building a lifetime career as a stabilizer within the framework of a single organization. Those who join companies with PFW intentions usually compete with those inside the company for better positions. They need not worry so much about outsiders who might be hired to fill positions they aspire to. Theoretically, everyone has a chance to compete, despite differences in education and experience. When someone at the top retires, a chain reaction can open up many positions all the way down the organizational ladder. This, of course, is possible only if reorganization does not take place or certain positions are not eliminated.

Organizations with PFW policies usually provide good training for their employees, so that they are ready to assume more responsibility when opportunities arise. This usually means that more on-the-job time is spent on training of all kinds. It also usually means that such companies will encourage their employees to continue their formal education and will often pay the bills. Because of this, employees are less likely to be ignored or lost in the shuffle.

Just as there are many advantages, there are also disadvantages, to working for a company that likes to promote from within. Many highly ambitious people claim that promotions come too slowly. People are trained too far ahead of time. There is too much waiting. These are usually the same people who claim that the best way to the top is to move from company to company instead of sticking it out with one organization. They point out that it is also possible that while waiting for an opening, a reorganization can take place, thus eliminating the position you were preparing to occupy. Moreover, the human-relations role is more critical because management and nonmanagement people seldom forget anything. In short, a person who makes a serious human-relations mistake inside a PFW company must live with it longer because the people affected will be around to remember.

In the rapidly changing present economic climate, organizations are beginning to realize that they must become more flexible if they are to remain profitable. In some cases, restructuring and massive layoffs have been necessary. As a result, the emphasis on PFW is much reduced; and in some organizations, it has been discarded.

The scrambling, or zigzag, route to the top involves an entirely different approach to career planning, as you can see from the following illustration. Here are some of the advantages of the scrambling approach.

1. For those who are willing to move about geographically and

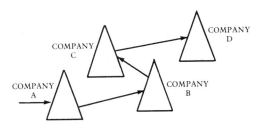

who are sufficiently aggressive to make the effort to seek out profitable transfers, the route to the top can be faster.

2. Sometimes an individual can achieve a wider and more valuable learning background by moving from one company to another. In other words, he or she can learn something new in each company and take it to the next one. This is especially true in high-technology fields.

3. It is easier to leave any serious human-relations mistakes behind and get a fresh start. This might include any unresolved human conflicts or personality differences.

There are also disadvantages to the zigzag route.

1. Most people agree that it takes more energy to build an industry-wide reputation to insure that profitable transfers come your way. There is also a degree of risk involved. You could discover, for example, that your most recent move was a mistake. Scramblers are not always successful.

2. Transferring often means uprooting the entire family and making profound personal and social, as well as professional, changes in your life.

3. Certain benefits, like profit sharing, cannot always be transferred from one company to another without a loss or adjustment.

As you plan your career, take the following human-relations factors into consideration.

- The longer you stay with a growing company, the more opportunities you will have, providing you continue to learn and to maintain good horizontal and vertical relationships.

- Moving horizontally into every possible department is a good idea, whether the move gives you an immediate pay increase or not. Not only will you improve your knowledge base, you will also be in a position to build new relationships that can help your career progress.

- Discover and study the various channels of promotion in your company. Attempt to move up through the channel that best suits your ability. Set the stage for this through your human-relations skills.

- Within bounds, do not fear being aggressive. Submit ideas that have been well researched. Communicate upward. Demonstrate your human-relations skills at every opportunity.

- When a position becomes vacant, let management know in the right way that you are interested. Do not assume that they know. It doesn't hurt your relationships with others to ask.

- Cultivate and maintain relationships outside your organization, especially with people in professional or trade organizations. If it becomes obvious that your organization cannot provide you with the growth opportunities you desire, these individuals can help you scramble.

Different Working Environments

It usually takes a few weeks before new employees are in a position to analyze their working environments and answer the following questions. Does this working environment (culture) fit my long-term needs? Is it within my personal comfort zone? Can I see myself moving up into more responsible positions?

In evaluating a working environment, the following need to be taken into consideration.

- Is there a profit-sharing or stock-option plan that causes employees to stay longer and be more protective of their respective roles and the firm as a whole?

- How stable is the organization? Is the firm strong enough to withstand being taken over by an outside firm? Is management sufficiently flexible to adjust to the economic winds of change?

- Is there a career class system within the organization? For example, hospitals have their medical doctors at one level, nurses at another, and nonprofessionals at another. Would you be comfortable under a similar environment?

- Would it bother you to work for an organization (i.e., restaurant) in which the steady turnover of employees makes it difficult to build long-term relationships?

- What about off-hour work? Hospitals, restaurants, and many factories have shift work that has a major impact on lifestyle.

- Would working in a high-fashion environment be in your comfort zone? Some retail organizations and home office centers create a *haute couture* that some enjoy but others do not.

Although the more investigation that takes place in advance the better, many new employees discover that the working environment they anticipated is not suitable for them. As a result, they develop a new career plan that will eventually take them into their comfort zone.

Having a Plan B

A professional scrambler always has a Plan B that he or she can put into operation when needed. A Plan B is a well-thought-out strategy (including an up-to-the-minute résumé, outside contacts, and constantly updated skills) that will permit the scrambler to locate a better position with another firm in the shortest possible time.

In the past, stabilizers have not felt the need to have a Plan B. There are two reasons why this is no longer viable. First, stabilizers have discovered that scramblers have often substantially improved their career positions by having and using a Plan B. Second, organizational changes (mergers, buy-outs, restructuring, etc.) have frequently left stabilizers holding the bag. Result? More and more stabilizers are going back to school to upgrade their skills and have a formal Plan B ready.

This author recommends that both scramblers and stabilizers develop a Plan B for two reasons.

1. If the winds of change eliminate your position you are prepared to move on to something better.

2. Just having a Plan B ready makes it easier for you to maintain a positive attitude where you are presently working.

Many workers become either discouraged with their progress or fearful that their jobs will be eliminated without doing anything about it. When they develop a Plan B they not only eliminate some of the fear that goes along with losing a job, but they feel better about their current positions, their attitudes improve, they become more productive, and they receive promotions. As a result, there is no need to scramble.

Problem 16

Preference

"I'm a stabilizer."

Angelo, an experienced technician, was forced into the labor market because of a major layoff. He was interviewed the same week by Company A and Company B. After more than two weeks of investigation, both firms offered him good jobs.

Company A is a dynamic, high-technology corporation that makes little effort to develop its own people. In fact, it takes great delight in hiring top people away from its competitors. Company A is interested in Angelo primarily because of his technical skills and the fact that he would become productive immediately.

Company B, on the other hand, is a technical organization that offers a great deal of security to employees because of its rather firm PFW policy. They like Angelo because of his technical abilities and long-range potential.

Although the starting salary with Company A is substantially higher, the training program with Company B is superior. *All other significant factors are similar.* Which company do you think Angelo should go with? What factors should he consider in making his decision? (For a suggested answer, see page 195.)

CHAPTER 17

KEEPING A POSITIVE ATTITUDE THROUGH PLATEAU PERIODS AND REORGANIZATIONS

Keeping a positive attitude takes on a new dimension when an ambitious employee reaches a plateau period in his climb up the corporate ladder. (A *plateau* is a long waiting period in which the role and the responsibility of the employee remain static.) Small automatic or cost-of-living pay increases may occur, but significant jumps do not. Sometimes plateau periods can last for years.

Why are they so difficult to live through?

In the first place, business and industry seem to intensify the problem because they seek out and hire highly ambitious people. They want and need dynamic men and women. They want and need people with energy. Because of this they often imply that personal progress will be swift and regular.

But after employment it is often necessary to turn around and ask these same ambitious people to be patient.

> "It takes time in any organization, Laura. Your day will come. Just sit tight and *wait*. You'll see."

> "You are doing great, Joe. Just *wait* for the right opportunity and you'll be off and running."

> "Continue to prepare, Henry. Learn all you can in your present job. You are in a plateau period, but you will get your chance. Just *wait* and see."

The "patience suit" that management people suggest other employees wear during plateau periods becomes too tight, too confining, too uncomfortable. When this happens, even confirmed stabilizers may consider scrambling to another firm.

Patience isn't something one learns in school or college. Indeed, the pattern of almost automatic promotions in school is the direct opposite of the pattern found in the world of work. Through our school systems, people become accustomed to promotions according to age. They start at the first grade and move up to the twelfth and beyond like clockwork—each year a step up, until regular promotions are expected without waiting. Small wonder that some people begin to think that life is one progressive step after another whether the step has been truly earned or not.

Our society contributes in other ways to this "make it in a hurry" attitude. Both economic and social upward mobility has been the pattern for most Americans in the past few generations. As a result, most young people whose parents have "made it" have been raised in an affluent environment. Why should they wait for thirty years to get to the same point? Why should they wait until they're ready to retire to make it, when they might do it by the time they're thirty?

Yet, when they get their first job, many young people must start at the bottom, with a relatively low income and no fixed promotion schedule to depend upon. Small wonder that many become impatient and seek shortcuts to better positions and higher incomes.

There are many reasons for plateau periods. The following quotations from three ambitious individuals are examples.

"I work for a fine company, but we have been undergoing an unavoidable retrenchment program for over three years. There has been a freeze on new hires and promotions. I think things will open up soon but, believe me, it has not been easy to readjust my personal goals and keep my attitude from showing."

"In our organization everyone must sweat out a long plateau between junior- and middle-management roles. I have had three front-line supervisory roles over the past few years, each with more responsibility. My next jump will be into middle management. But there are many people waiting ahead of me. If I could make a move to a competing company, I might save myself a few years of waiting."

"I was all set to move into a role I had spent three years preparing for, when my organization went through a consolidation period and transferred the position I wanted to another city. Not wishing to move there, I had to readjust my goals. So here I am, in another plateau period."

Even if things could be normal inside business organizations, which is seldom the case, promotions are not automatic. Plateaus still exist. So how is one to cope?

First, the ambitious employee should learn as much as possible about plateaus so that he (or she) can see the value of staying positive during such periods. Second, he should study ways in which such periods can be shortened.

Business and industrial leaders believe in *promotion by merit.* They know that the opportunity to succeed in open competition with others provides the vitality their organizations must have. Seniority, experience, minority status, and age are not always enough to win a given promotion. Capability must also be demonstrated. But even the most capable employees reach plateaus. The opportunities to move up still exist, of course, but they sometimes come only after long periods of waiting.

- These periods of waiting are critical.

- They can destroy confidence.

- They can create problems.

But far more important than all other factors is what happens to the attitude of the employee during such periods of waiting. Here is what frequently happens.

When employees who are living through a plateau period permit their attitudes to turn negative, they defeat themselves. At the very point when management is watching and they should be working up to their potential, they let things fall apart. When this happens, the plateau is often extended, and others, who have a better hold on their attitude, are given the promotional opportunities that exist. Another way of saying this is that an ambitious employee cannot afford the "luxury of being bored."

It is not an easy thing to ask an aggressive person to remain positive and wait, but there often is no alternative. Opportunities can and do open up in organizations overnight, but it is almost impossible to produce a steady flow of opportunities to fit the time schedules of individuals.

Management cannot eliminate all the pressure points that an employee stuck on a plateau faces. Management people can, however, understand the frustration that comes when a promising career gets temporarily bogged down. They know because they have usually been there themselves. They know it is a difficult period. They know it is a time when some people begin seriously to question their goals. They know it is a time when personal values are challenged. They know it is a time when some start to think about other careers or returning to college for more formal education.

Being ambitious and capable has never been easy in our society. When employees are in their twenties, a year may seem more like five years. And yet many employees are past thirty before they have an opportunity to demonstrate fully their true ability.

True, a few people do find success early. The entertainment field, professional sports, sales, and promotional activities, for example, may give the young person with talent, ability, and desire an early break.

At first, it appears that professional people also achieve their goals early in life. However, it is easy to forget that those who build careers in medicine, engineering, law, and the other professions must invest more time in their formal education. Physicians are often close to thirty when they start their practices. The same is true for lawyers, engineers, and other professionals.

Understanding plateau periods may help an ambitious employee do a better job of coping, but aren't there ways to shorten them? Should you be faced with a plateau period in the future, please ask yourself these questions:

Am I using my present role to improve my future, whether or not I stay with the organization? Some people have the capacity to turn boring jobs into self-improvement periods. A good example might be the ambitious supervisor of a shipping operation who wants to know more about data processing. On company time she (or he) might start investigating the possibilities for her own department, thereby benefiting both her department and herself.

Am I taking advantage of all the training opportunities available to me now? Such opportunities could be both inside and outside the company walls. A community involvement of any kind can help one live through or even shorten a plateau period. Many employees have found moonlighting both therapeutic and financially rewarding.

Is it time to revise my career goals? When organizations change internally, employees must adjust. Instead of resisting changes, they must turn them into opportunities. For example, you might consider changing your channel of promotion by asking for a transfer to a growing, instead of a declining, department.

Have I applied for a promotion? Upward communication to let management know you feel you are ready for more responsibility is often worthwhile, even if nothing happens. It may not eliminate a plateau, but it could shorten it.

Are there some company-sponsored activities I could become involved in? Often there are sports activities, study groups, and cultural programs that can give you additional employee and management contacts as well as pleasure. Such activities may not shorten plateau periods, but they may make them seem shorter.

What about doing something spectacular? Is it possible that you could volunteer for a very tough assignment that nobody else has been willing to tackle? This could provide you with a personal challenge. It could also communicate a great deal to upper management about your potential and readiness to accept more responsibility.

There are many other action steps people can take to shorten plateau periods, or at least make them easier to live through. There are also cases where the employee should not live through them but rather adopt the zigzag route to the top and initiate a move to another organization. In contemplating such action, please keep the following three points in mind. They will help you remain positive.

1. The first years with an organization should be viewed as an apprenticeship. The training and experience must be considered the plus factor during this period. The employee is serving an internship similar to that in the medical profession.

2. Many employees have received promotions before they were ready, and their careers have been permanently damaged. Will you be sufficiently trained for a good opportunity when it

does come? Will you be ready for the responsibility? Will you be sufficiently mature to handle it? "Too much too soon" could be a real threat to your long-range goal.

3. Although few people question the fact that personal advancement is often slow during the starting years, they seldom point out that the tempo of personal progress can increase greatly in later years. This is one reason why you should not set up a personal timetable for yourself. Progress may be slow at the start of your career but very fast later. Yes, set a goal for yourself, but do not expect that goal to arrive exactly according to your time schedule. It may not fit that of your organization.

If you do set your own time schedule and management is unable to meet it, then you may lose your positive attitude. This loss will hurt you as well as the company. The future of any company cannot be charted in detail many years in advance.

Today — more than during any previous period — organizations are going through restructuring programs. Sometimes such changes create waiting periods, cause reassignments, even layoffs. At other times, reorganizations create opportunities for those alert enough to perceive them. Not all changes are predictable. Not all changes can be converted into career opportunities. But some are — and it is your job to be ready when they occur. Ready and waiting. Staying positive as you live through plateaus can be the greatest human-relations challenge you face. That is why more and more professionals are developing a Plan B.

Problem 17

Change

"I hate change."

In a company-sponsored seminar devoted to how to handle and adjust to change, Jane made this statement to the group: "When it comes to the future and the changes it may bring, I believe that the Protestant ethic of hard work plus sound human-relations techniques will see me through. If my present superiors do not recognize and reward me, then someone else will."

The following response came from Darlene, a co-worker and good friend of Jane's: "I think it is comfortable for Jane to have so much faith in hard work and human-relations skills, but I think that adapting to change requires a more aggressive and creative approach. Jane, with her somewhat naive attitude, may be left behind. It has been my practice to try to turn change into opportunity through action. When a change occurs, I sit back for a day or so and figure out how I can convert the change to my advantage and enhance my career. At such a critical juncture, I cannot rely on past performance and routine human relations. I must shift gears and look out for #1, even if it means temporarily stepping on the feelings of others. When change comes, it is not business as usual. I cannot prevent or control change, but if I am clever, I can turn it to my advantage."

Who, in your opinion, is best prepared to handle the dramatic changes most experts claim will occur in the future, Jane or Darlene? Is there a better strategy? (For a suggested answer, see page 195.)

CHAPTER **18**

"I'm ready for a fresh start."

WHEN YOU ARE TEMPTED TO SCRAMBLE

Freedom to accept or resign a job, seek employment in a certain career field, or join the organization of one's choice are important rights. They should be appreciated by all free people. But what does each of these rights mean to you, a member of the work force?

It means you can be a stabilizer and, providing you select the right firm, you can build your entire career inside a single organization. It means you can leave a position with a large or small organization and go into business for yourself. It means you can leave your present occupation and go back to school to prepare for a new career. It also means you may choose to become a scrambler and follow the zigzag route to the top by making a move to another organization every time you can substantially improve your situation. It means you can keep on switching jobs until you find the occupation or company that's right for you.

Some resignations are positive actions: they benefit both the organization and the individual. Some make sense because reorganizations increase the possibilities of future layoffs. Some resignations, for a variety of personal reasons, are unavoidable. Some, however, seem to stem from poor judgment and turn out to be mistakes.

There are dangers to any resignation. You could wind up with a job that is not as good as the one you left. You might even wind up temporarily stranded. Thousands of people leave organizations every year only to regret it later. The pastures in another occupational area or company may, from a distance, look greener than they really are. Resigning a position, whether you have a door open elsewhere or not, is a serious step. Careful research is recommended.

When, then, should you resign a position?

As a general rule, you should resign when you have been *unhappy and unproductive for a considerable length of time.* Under such conditions, your career with the company has already been seriously damaged. A new start in a new environment would most likely be to your advantage.

People who are ambitious should look elsewhere for employment when they discover they have not been working close to their potential for a long time. They should seek opportunities elsewhere when their productivity has been down for months and they can't get it back up. They should consider other options when their attitude has been negative for a long time and they do not seem to be able to do anything about it.

Surveys and statistics show, however, that most resignations are not due to the preceding reasons, *but are based primarily upon personality conflicts and human problems.* Rather than leaving for a better position, people are getting *away* from the frustrations of their present job. Because such problems can frequently be solved, or at least made less traumatic, it would appear that many people resign their positions for the wrong reasons. In other words, leaving a job because it is not the right one for you is one thing. Leaving a job because of human-relations incompetencies is something else.

To help you avoid these and other mistakes, here are some questions to ask yourself when considering a resignation.

Are you resigning under emotional stress?

We are all tempted to chuck a job when everything seems to be going wrong or when we are frustrated and emotionally upset. It is a natural reaction. A resignation, however, should be a rational decision based upon many facts and should be made only after long, careful analysis and planning.

It is difficult to think clearly and logically when you are emotionally disturbed about a human-relations problem that cannot be quickly solved. During these periods, back away from such a serious decision. Sleep on it. Talk to a third person. Give it time. Make another, more serious attempt to solve it. A resignation should not be an impulsive decision. In the majority of cases, it is irrevocable.

Are you resigning because of a personality conflict?

Resigning because of a single personality conflict can seriously hamper a promising career. This is not to say that such conflicts do not occur. They do. But they can usually be resolved with time and effort. Give someone in authority a chance to help. Give time a chance to help. Most of all, be honest with yourself and ask whether you can afford to let one person destroy a promising career — especially when it is yours.

Are you marking time?

Frequently, highly capable employees sense that they are not "going anywhere" in their present jobs, yet they do nothing to find a better opportunity. Such individuals often drag along for years doing both themselves and their firms a disservice. Later you hear them say: "I should have made a change years ago!" Facing such a negative career situation head-on may be justified to avoid having the penalties and regrets of lack-of-progress later.

Have you talked your situation over with your supervisor or the person who hired you?

Many employees are fearful of talking over a possible resignation with a management person. Some believe that it will be held against them if they voice their dissatisfaction. They feel that their chances of finding a better job elsewhere will be weakened. Some feel it would be an act of disloyalty. Others feel it to be a waste of time.

Whatever your reason, you would be wise not to resign until you have discussed the problem with your supervisor or someone in personnel or upper management. A twenty-minute discussion with the right person has stopped many a foolish resignation. Many problems can be resolved through free and open communication with management. Give those in charge a chance to help you resolve your problem before you take final action. You have nothing to lose. You could even discover that the position that you are thinking of leaving has more potential than any you could find elsewhere.

Are you resigning to save face?

Everyone makes mistakes. Sometimes you may overcommit yourself or take a stand on an issue that you feel you cannot back away from. Resigning on this basis can be a mistake, especially if you have exaggerated the difficulty of the adjustment. It may be better to admit such a mistake than to pay a price out of all proportions. Such a resignation might be harmful to both your future and the company's.

Have you exhausted all opportunities to learn more where you are?

A key factor in any decision to resign should be whether you can continue to grow in your present job. If you are completely boxed in with no opportunity to improve yourself, then you should certainly consider a change. If, however, you can continue to learn while waiting for a break, your situation is not as bad as it could be.

Are you working close to your potential?

Your future depends on your having a position in a company where you can work close to your potential. If the gap between what you are capable of doing and your current level of productivity is too wide, your career progress may be stalled. You must be able to use your ability, aptitude, and talent to a reasonable extent. You must be productive to succeed. You must find a way to contribute.

Your company is entitled to the best in you. If you find your position doesn't bring out the best in you, then it isn't fair to either you or the company for you to remain. You should find something more suitable. An employee who is not productive is doing herself (or himself) and her company more harm than good.

If, after serious consideration of all the preceding questions you decide to resign in the best interests of both parties, how should you go about it? Here are a few tips on how to resign gracefully.

Resign on a face-to-face basis. It is good human relations to go to the person who hired you, as well as to your supervisor, and resign face to face. A letter of resignation or a telephone resignation alone may leave a bad impression that could hurt you later. You will gain the respect of management when you resign in person. You will feel better, too.

Tell management the real reasons for your resignation. It may be difficult for you to reveal the actual causes for your leaving, but you should do so anyway. Reliable information of this kind can lead to changes that will benefit those you leave behind. Honesty is always the best human-relations policy.

Give ample notice. Be sure that you give at least the traditional two weeks' notice. This amount of time may be necessary for the company to recruit and train a replacement.

Continue to be productive. Don't take advantage of the fact that you are leaving. You will gain respect from others, as well as personal satisfaction, by working hard up to the very last hour. This is one way to leave a clean record behind you.

Turn in all equipment. All company equipment, down to the most minute item, should be officially turned in through regular channels.

Transfer all responsibilities to your replacement gracefully. Give the person taking over your job a break. Give her (or him) all possible help and assistance. Try not to leave her with any problems you can take care of before leaving. Transfer to her, as far as possible, any good relationships you have developed.

Swallow any last-minute negative comments. There is a temptation for some people to become negative and pour out their hostilities before they have turned in their resignations. Resist any vindictive instincts you may have.

Moving on for the right reasons. Those who move on for the right reasons — opportunity to use new knowledge, gain broader experience, improve career status and financial benefits — avoid the consequences of repeating human-relationship mistakes and communicating instability on their job applications.

Always resign a position in such a manner that you will feel free to seek reemployment there at a later date. You are the sum total of all your experiences. When you leave a job, you do not leave emptyhanded. You take your experience and training with you. And you take the knowledge you've gained from all your human-relations experiences. Such knowledge is never without value. Make that known. Leave on the right foot.

A shopping-center manager recently made this statement: "One of the most important things I learned in college was to anticipate and be willing to accept change. I expected I would walk into a dynamic, changing world—I was not prepared for the turmoil that really exists. Many outstanding people are left unemployed through no fault of their own."

Like other things in life, organizations grow, decline, go through management shake-ups, and sometimes change owner-ship. The fear of a possible layoff, relocation, or adjustment to a new work environment and superior can turn an upbeat, produc-tive employee into a negative one.

How would you protect your positive attitude under the preceding circumstances? Here are a few tips.

- Your positive attitude belongs to *you*, not your company. It is a priceless personal possession, so protect it for your own happiness. As you do this, keep in mind that a rumor about an organizational change is still a rumor until verified and a definite change in your status has been made. Contrary to popular belief, the majority of ownership changes do not re-sult in layoffs and significant adjustments among lower-level managers and employees.

- To help keep you positive, start a Plan B. Whether a forced change is coming or not, it is always a sound idea to explore other options through a Plan B. Upgrade your skills where you are, so you can be a winner no matter what happens.

- Don't take organizational restructuring personally. A com-pany sale or change of ownership may appear to be a cold, calculated business decision, but it is transacted within the same free enterprise system in which the company was created and nurtured in the first place. It is unfortunate when job losses occur, but neither you nor anyone else is to blame. Focus on the fact that, if you keep your positive attitude, a prospective employer will likely see you as a lucky find. Sometimes unwelcome change leads an individual with the right attitude to a superior career role.

- Remember that it does not hurt your reputation to be caught in a situation where an organizational change forces you into a career move. It is discouraging enough to go through any adjustment caused by a change in ownership. If you lose your positive attitude along with it, you are a double loser. Stay objective and professional. If it is to your advantage, go out and find yourself a more rewarding position!

Problem 18

Interview

"Attitude makes the difference."

Mark was deeply discouraged for two reasons. First, his present job was intolerable. Second, he had had seven job interviews in the past three months, but he had received little positive response from any and no job offers.

Mark felt his discouragement was justified. He had been trying extremely hard and had followed sound job-seeking practices. He had done advance research on all the organizations ahead of the interview. He was meticulous in his grooming. He was careful in completing the application blank and always made certain to submit a resume along with it. In addition to all this, it was clear that he had more than the minimum qualifications for all the positions for which he applied.

What was wrong?

Mark decided to discuss his problem with a very perceptive placement director. Together they came to the conclusion that Mark was not coming through or transmitting his best attitude during the interview period. In other words, he was losing out to other applicants because he was not communicating well. Were his answers too low key? Or too brief? Was he nervous? What might he do to sell himself to the interviewers without overdoing it, coming on too strong, or being phoney?

Because you went through a successful interview recently and were offered a new position with a substantial increase in pay and responsibility, Mark comes to you for assistance. He asks you four typical questions, ones that he has been encountering in his interviews. He wants to measure the way you handle them and then compare your responses to his own. He wants to model his replies after yours. This will, in turn, improve his personal confidence and help him communicate his true worth as a prospective employee.

Because Mark is a good friend, you decide to help him out. Now, in order to provide the maximum assistance you agree to do one of the following: (1) Actually role play the situation and reply to the following questions in class to the best of your ability. Assume all other factors (application, grooming, and so forth) are up to standard and that you are fully qualified for the hypothetical position; (2) Write out, word for word, the way you would reply to each of the following questions:

a. What made you decide you would like to work for our company?

b. What do you feel you will be able to contribute to our organization?

c. What human-relations skills will you bring with you?

d. Why have you decided to leave your present organization?

e. What are some of your weaknesses?

(For suggested answers, see page 196.)

CHAPTER **19**

"Something needs adjusting."

ATTITUDE
RENEWAL

Renewal means to restore or refresh. Employees at all levels occasionally need to renew their positive view toward their careers, rejuvenate their approach to the type of work they perform, or reestablish their positive focus toward their organizations. Everyone, even the most optimistic individual, should, from time to time, go through some form of attitude renewal. To some, maintaining a "positive focus" is a full-time job.

Attitude renewal, at the first level, is often a daily process. For a few, moments of early-morning meditation is helpful. Others, who may get off to a bad start, call a friend mid-morning for a "boost" and then start the day anew. Other forms of adjustment (regaining a positive focus) can take place at other points all through a given day.

At a more serious level attitude renewal can be a "weekend project." You hear both employees and managers make statements such as: "I need a strong dose of weekend rest and recreation to get my attitude ready for Monday morning." "Without the quiet time I enjoy during weekends, I would be a basket case Monday morning." Without periodic time off or weekend attitude adjustment periods, most people could not remain positive and productive in their work environments.

There are times, however, when even weekend renewals are not sufficient. A major overhaul may be necessary. This is true because now and then most individuals fall into an "attitudinal rut."

167

An attitudinal rut usually occurs when someone slips unknowingly into a pattern of negative behavior that, unfortunately, can continue over a long period of time. Although some days are better than others, the individual's focus is permanently skewed to the negative side of his or her perception. Obviously, remaining in an attitudinal rut can inflict severe damage on one's career.

Nevertheless, it is possible to fall into such a rut without knowing it. When you become physically ill, for example, your body sends you a signal — you get a headache, a fever, or pain — and you do something about it. When you slip into an attitudinal rut, your mind may be unable to send you a clear signal of distress because it does not inflict physical pain. Your co-workers or close friends may *want* to send you a signal, but it is such a sensitive area, they back away. As a consequence, some people stay in their attitudinal ruts for long periods.

> Over two years ago, when he was passed over for a promotion he thought he deserved, George pushed himself into a negative rut. He is in the same trough today. If there were some easy way to tell George he is negative, he would deny it because he has been in his special rut so long he thinks his behavior is normal. As a result, he cannot see he is his own worst enemy.

Attitude and Stress

Job stress is self-imposed when workers set too many difficult goals for themselves, and, as a result, move in an unorganized manner in too many directions at the same time. Most stress, however, is caused by the job itself. Some jobs — such as those of television news personnel, air traffic controllers, and police officers — are recognized as stressful. Excessive stress can cause job burnout, which results in impairment of work productivity. Warning signals include feelings of frustration (Chapter 9), emotional outbursts, and withdrawal. Human relationships usually deteriorate.

Do those who maintain positive attitudes handle stress better than others? Generally speaking, yes. When you focus on the positive elements of a work environment, you are more apt to envision yourself as a winner. Result? You laugh more and find it easier to relax. Under these behavioral patterns, less stress impacts upon the individual and the stress that does is dissipated with less damage. In contrast, those with behavioral patterns connected with negative attitudes appear to "open the door" to additional stress and hold the pressure created within themselves longer.

Although the more stress that can be removed from any job (fewer deadlines, unreasonable demands, and human conflicts) the better, all jobs generate some stress. Whatever the stress level may be, those who concentrate on maintaining good co-worker relationships seem to handle it with less harm to themselves.

Can returning to a positive from a negative attitude be considered an antidote to excessive stress and possible burnout? To a limited extent, yes. When excessive stress eventually "gets to" workers, they often focus excessively on the negative factors always present. After an attitude-renewal program takes place (vacation, counseling, self-help), these same people see the more positive factors present; in this sense, returning to their positive attitude constitutes an antidote.

The Attitude Adjustment Scale that follows is designed to help you assess the current condition of your own attitude. View it in the same manner you would one of those electronic instruments used to determine if your car engine needs a tune-up. The results might send you a signal that, with a few adjustments, you could be a more positive, successful, and happy person.

ATTITUDE ADJUSTMENT SCALE

Please use this exercise to rate your current attitude. Read the statement and circle the number where you feel you belong. If you circle a 10, you are saying your attitude could not be better in this area; if you circle a 1, you are saying it could not be worse.

	High (Positive)	Low (Negative)

1. I'm not going to ask, but my honest guess is that my boss would now rate my general attitude as . . . 10 9 8 7 6 5 4 3 2 1

	High (Positive)	Low (Negative)
2. Given a chance, co-workers and family would rate my attitude as a . . .	10 9 8 7 6 5 4 3 2 1	
3. I would rate my attitude as a . . .	10 9 8 7 6 5 4 3 2 1	
4. In dealing with others, I believe my current effectiveness rates a . . .	10 9 8 7 6 5 4 3 2 1	
5. My current creativity level rates . . .	10 9 8 7 6 5 4 3 2 1	
6. If there were a meter to gauge my sense of humor at this stage, I believe it would read close to a . . .	10 9 8 7 6 5 4 3 2 1	
7. My recent disposition — the patience and sensitivity I show to others — deserves a rating of . . .	10 9 8 7 6 5 4 3 2 1	
8. For not letting little things bother me recently, I deserve a . . .	10 9 8 7 6 5 4 3 2 1	
9. Based on the number of compliments I've received lately, I deserve a . . .	10 9 8 7 6 5 4 3 2 1	
10. I would rate my enthusiasm toward my job and life in general during the past few weeks as a . . .	10 9 8 7 6 5 4 3 2 1	
Total	_____	

A score of 90 or over is a signal that your attitude is "in tune," and no adjustments are necessary; a score between 70 and 90 is a signal that minor adjustments may help; if you rated yourself under 50, a complete overhaul may be required.

Regardless of how you rated yourself on the scale, the attitude-adjustment techniques that follow can help you become a more positive and effective individual.

Adjustment 1
Employ the Flip Side Technique

The pivotal factor between being positive or negative is often a sense of humor. Attitude and humor have a symbiotic relationship. The more you develop your sense of humor, the more positive you will become. The more positive you become, the better your sense of humor will be. It's a happy arrangement.

Some people successfully use the "flip-side technique" to maintain and enhance their sense of humor. When a "negative" enters their lives, they immediately flip the problem over (as you would a phonograph record) and look for whatever humor may exist on the other side. When they succeed, these clever individuals are able to minimize the negative impact the problem has on their positive attitude.

> Jim, a software spreadsheet specialist, was devastated when he walked into his apartment. Everything was in shambles, and he quickly discovered some valuable possessions were missing. After assessing the situation, Jim called Mary and said: "I think I have figured out a way for us to take that vacation trip to Mexico. I've just been robbed, but my homeowners insurance is paid up. Why not come over and help me clean up while we finalize our plans?"

Humor, in any form, resists negative forces. It can restore your positive attitude and help you maintain a more balanced perspective on life.

How do you define a sense of humor?

A sense of humor is an attitudinal quality (mental focus) that encourages an individual to discover humor others may not see in the same situation. It is a philosophy that says: "If you take life too seriously, it will pull you down. Force yourself to pull back and laugh at the human predicament."

Countless incidents, which you could improve with a humorous twist, occur in your life each day. They will pass you by, however, unless you educate your attitude to see them. To help you do this, it might be helpful to give this mental set a special name. My nomination is "funny focus." It may sound frivolous, but it describes what some wise people are actually able to do.

> "Susan always adjusts more quickly because she directs that strange mind of hers to the funny side."

> "Sam is good company because he has the unique capacity to find humor in any situation."

Those who receive such compliments nurture a "funny focus" that permits them to create a more positive perspective. This focus is their antidote to negative situations.

How can you improve your attitude through a greater sense of humor? How can you develop a funny focus that will fall within your comfort zone? Recognizing the following should help.

Humor is an inside job. Humor is not something that is natural for one person and unnatural for another. One individual is not blessed with a reservoir of humor waiting to be released while another is left to cry. A sense of humor is created. With practice anyone can do it.

Laughter is therapeutic. Just as negative emotions such as tension, anger, or stress can produce ulcers, headaches, and high blood pressure, positive emotions can relax nerves, improve digestion and circulation, and otherwise contribute to physical and emotional wellness. Dr. William F. Fry, Jr., a psychiatrist and associate clinical professor at Stanford University Medical School, maintains: "Laughter gets the endocrine system going." Of course, you can't laugh away all serious problems, but you can laugh your way into a more positive focus to help you cope with the problem. Laughter is soul music to attitude. It is a way of adjustment to a funny focus.

A funny focus can get you out of the problem and into the solution. Finding the humor in a situation usually won't solve a problem but it can lead you in the right direction. Laughing can help transfer your focus from the problem to the solution. Using the flip-side technique starts the process.

Adjustment 2
Play Your Winners

When retailers discover a certain item is selling faster than others, they pour additional promotional money into this product. Their motto is: "Play the winners—don't go broke trying to promote the losers."

This same approach can help you adjust and maintain a positive attitude. You have special winners in your life. *The more you focus on them the better.*

Jason, at this point in his life, has more losers than winners. Having spent ten years in the work force, he is currently adjusting to a divorce, is deeply in debt, and his car is giving him fits. The only two positive factors are his job (Jason is making progress in the hotel management field he loves) and running. By pouring his energies into his career, plus running a minimum of six miles each day, Jason is able to maintain a positive attitude. He is playing his winners.

Each of us — at any stage in our lives — must deal with both positive factors (winners) and negative factors (losers). If not constantly alert, losers can take over and push your winners out of your mental focus. When this happens, you spend "mind time" dwelling on your losers. Allowed to continue, your attitude will become negative, and your disposition will turn sour. *Your challenge is to find ways to push the losers to the perimeter of your thinking* where you can live with them, perhaps permanently, in a graceful manner.

How can you do this?

Here are three simple suggestions:

THINK more about your winners. The more you concentrate on the winning elements in your life, the less time you will have to devote to the negative. This means that your negative factors will receive less attention and, as a result, many may resolve themselves.

TALK only about your winners. As long as you don't overdo it (or repeat yourself with the same party), the more you verbalize the happy, exciting factors in your life, the more important they become to you. Those who talk incessantly about the negative aspects of their lives do their friends a disservice and perpetuate their own negative attitude.

REWARD yourself by enjoying your winners. If you enjoy nature, play this winner by taking a nature walk. If music is a positive influence, listen to your favorite artist. If religion is a powerful force in your life, play your winner by praying.

You play your winners every time you think or talk or pray about them. But obviously the best thing you can do is *enjoy* them. If you are a golfer, playing eighteen holes will do more for your attitude than thinking or talking about doing it.

Adjustment 3
Give Your Positive Attitude to Others

When you get fed up with the behavior of others, you may be tempted to tell them off and give them "a piece of your mind." This is understandably human. It is a better policy, however, to give others "a piece of your positive attitude." When you do this, you permit others to help you adjust your attitude.

> Sharon asked Casey to meet her for lunch because she needed a psychological lift. Casey didn't feel much like it, but she accepted and made a special effort to be upbeat. When the luncheon was over, Casey had not only given Sharon a boost, she felt better herself. Both parties came out ahead.

When you give part of your positive attitude to others, you create a symbiotic relationship. The recipient feels better, but so do you. In a somewhat upside-down twist, *you keep your positive attitude by giving it away.*

Everyone has opportunities to give their positive attitude to others. Taxi drivers who make their passengers laugh will increase their tips; employees who give co-workers deserved compliments increase their popularity; homeowners who send positive signals to neighbors thus eliminate problems with them when they see them, vacationers can enhance their fun by making new friends simply by being pleasant to fellow travelers. Opportunities abound. The results are best, however, when the giving is toughest.

> It has been a difficult Friday for Jane. Due to an emergency staff meeting in the morning, she was behind in her work. Just as she was starting to catch up, the computer went down. Then her boss asked her to finish an unexpected project before leaving for the weekend. When she finally left work, all Jane could think of was getting in her jacuzzi and forgetting it all. But she had promised herself to visit her friend, Jackie, who was hospitalized. The temptation to drive straight home was strong, but she resisted and made her visit. An hour later Jane arrived home refreshed and positive. She didn't need the jacuzzi.

Each individual winds up a winner by giving his or her positive attitude away in a manner suited to his or her own personal style.

Adjustment 4
Look Better to Yourself

You are constantly bombarded through media advertising to improve your image. Most messages state that only with a "new look" can you find acceptance and meet new friends.

> "Discover the new you. Join our health club and expand your circle of friends."

"Let plastic surgery help you find a new partner."

Self-improvement of any kind should be applauded; but the overriding reason for a "new image" is not to look better for others, but for yourself. When you improve your appearance, you give your positive attitude a boost. It is not what happens outside that counts, but how your mind sees yourself.

The term *inferiority complex* is not in popular use today; however, I still relish this old textbook definition: *An inferiority complex is said to occur when you look better to others than you do to yourself.* In other words, when you have a negative self-image, you *make* yourself feel psychologically inferior, when you probably are not.

The truth is that you often do look better to others than you do to yourself. There may be periods when you feel unfashionable, unattractive and dowdy—but this does not mean you look that way to your friends. The problem is that you are communicating a negative attitude because you don't look good to yourself.

When you have a poor self-image, it is as though you are looking through a glass darkly. You feel you don't look good, so nothing else looks good to you. This occurs because your negative image psychologically distorts your attitude (the way you look at things mentally).

You see yourself first, your environment second. You can't remove yourself from the perceptual process.

> Cedric gave up on ever having a good self-image when he was a teenager. All through college he was considered a reclusive grind. Approaching graduation, Cedric enrolled in a noncredit course designed to prepare students for a professional job-search. Part of the program included doing a mock-employment interview on video tape that would be critiqued by the instructor and fellow students. To prepare for this unwanted ordeal, Cedric purchased a new suit, had his hair restyled, and bought new, more fashionable glass frames. He practiced over and over at home. When his day arrived, Cedric did so well he received compliments from all who viewed the tape. This recognition and support had a wonderful impact on Cedric. For the first time, he looked good to himself. Cedric's negative image was no longer a barrier to a good future.

The connection between a good self-image and a positive attitude cannot be ignored. In keeping a better image, it will help if you: (1) admit that at times you may look better to others than you look to yourself; (2) play up your winning features — hair, smile, eyes, etc.; and (3) make improvements in grooming — when improvement is possible.

Adjustment 5
Accept the Physical Connection

Apparently no one has been able to prove conclusively that there is a direct relationship between physical well-being and attitude. Most, however, including the most cynical of researchers in the area, concede there is a connection.

More than any previous generation, today's young adults are aware of physical fitness. A surprising number incorporate daily workouts into their schedules. Their commitment to the "attitude connection" is expressed in these typical comments.

"My workout does as much for my attitude as it does for my body."

"Exercise tones up my body and tunes up my outlook."

"I never underestimate what working out does for me psychologically."

Many fitness enthusiasts depend upon exercise to keep them out of attitudinal ruts.

"I've renamed my health club The Attitude Adjustment Factory."

"I take a long walk to push negative thoughts out of my system."

"An unusually tough workout will often get me out of a mental rut."

No single group in our society deals more with the psychological aspects of attitude than professional athletes. Increasingly, athletes engage year-round in sophisticated physical conditioning programs. They realize they must stay in shape to remain competitive.

"This same football team finished in the cellar last year. We made the play-offs this year because we have a new team attitude."

"I owe my success this season to my wife. She helped me adjust my attitude."

"My success this year is 90 percent due to a better attitude."

They must be trying to tell us something.

Problem 19

Focus

"I'll adjust later."

Lupe is suffering from the "campus blahs." With finals only a few weeks away, Lupe has lost her motivation to excel. Everything is a drag. Could it be excessive study time? A demanding part-time job? Home problems? Whatever the reason, she is even discouraged with her personal image. Why must life be so out of focus?

Jack appears to be "approaching career burnout." A very hard-working, highly successful professional sales representative, Jack senses he has lost "touch" with customers. For the first time they are reacting to his approach negatively. Despite his need for more money to cover new personal financial commitments, his commission check last month was lower. Even his daily jogging is not helping him maintain a positive attitude. Why are things so out of focus?

Would you recommend the five adjustment techniques to both Lupe and Jack? Which do you think would help Lupe the most? Jack? Why? (For a suggested answer, see page 197.)

CHAPTER **20**

"Being a supervisor can
be a big headache."

SHOULD YOU BECOME A MANAGER OR A LEADER?

Congratulations! By improving your human-relations skills and achieving greater insight into your positive attitude, you now possess the foundation upon which you can build a more promising career. Such a career may lead you into business management or a leadership role in a different career area of your choice. No one I know will argue with the following statements.

The more you practice sound human relations as an employee, the more likely it is that your superiors will promote you into management.

Everything you learn and practice about attitude and good human relations now will help you achieve a leadership position later.

Wherever you may be employed now or in the future, your superiors will probably be sensitive to the fact that you are building and maintaining better relationships with people than your co-workers and that you know how to operate effectively in a group — that you have a double competency. You are skillful technically. You are also skillful with people. Observing this double competency, your superiors will naturally assume that if you are good at human relations at the employee level, you will also be good at the management level. It is a wise assumption. Let's look at what happened to Cleo.

A highly competent word-processor operator, Cleo concentrated on her personal productivity, but she did not neglect her human-relations skills. She would frequently stop her own work to help someone with a problem. She would sometimes pitch in at the end of the day to help others get out an urgent report. Her efforts to help her co-workers did not go unrecognized.

Cleo was invited to attend a supervisory course on company time. Two weeks after the course was over, she became a supervisor. She was elated, not only because she had very little seniority, but also because she was the youngest person in her department. Her quick promotion made her respect her human-relations skills more than ever.

The best thing about becoming more human-relations competent is that it makes one more self-confident. It happens every time. In short, the more you practice the human-relations skills discussed in this book, the more self-confidence you will build. Learning to establish strong working relationships with those who are older and more experienced than you is confidence building; being able to restore a damaged relationship is confidence building. The more you can prove to yourself that you are good at people skills, the less likely it is that you will be intimidated by others. Soon you will discover that you can deal effectively with sophisticated, experienced superiors at all levels; soon you will feel sufficiently confident to step out in front and be a leader. Jerry is a good case in point.

Jerry, a sensitive and quiet young man, completed a self-study course in human relations because he wanted to develop more meaningful relationships with people both on and off the job. It was a personal thing with Jerry. He had no thoughts of ever becoming a leader. Such a role, he thought, was beyond his capacity. Yet inside of two years Jerry was so good at building relationships with co-workers that his personal confidence tripled. To both management and fellow workers he became a different person. When he was invited to become a supervisor, the only one surprised was Jerry himself.

When you demonstrate the self-confidence that practicing good human relations produces, new career doors automatically open. You may or may not choose to enter such doors, but it will be personally rewarding to know they are open.

Your transition into a supervisory role should be smooth because all the human-relations competencies you practice as an employee can be transferred to your new role. In fact, some skills will make more sense to you as a supervisor. For example, having tried, perhaps unsuccessfully, to build a relationship with a difficult supervisor, you will be more sensitive to the problem once you are there yourself. Knowing how a conflict between two co-workers can injure the productivity of all, you will pick up on such situations faster and intervene sooner. Knowing the rewards your supervisor could have given you but didn't, you will be more sensitive to your employees' need for recognition. This is what happened to Geraldine.

> Geraldine was so disturbed by the behavior and insensitivity of her supervisor that she swore she would never become one herself. Then, because of a dramatic change in her personal life, she had second thoughts. Her rationale was as follows: Because the managers in my field are so ineffective, the opportunities should be limitless for someone like me who is willing to learn how to be a good supervisor.
>
> So what did Geraldine do? She took a basic course in human-relations skills and another course in management. As she did this, she made mental notes of the skills she would employ that her present manager did not. Her opportunity came sooner than she anticipated, and because of her basic preparation, the transition was smooth. Geraldine has since received two additional promotions. What she learned as an employee provided her with a ticket to career success.

What about you? Should you, now that you are at least partly prepared, pursue a management role? If you are already in a beginning supervisor role, should you strike out for something in middle or upper management? The decision, of course, deserves careful consideration. Here are some thoughts you might wish to turn over in your mind.

Accept the edge you already possess, but admit you have much to learn. Many capable supervisors study human relations after they win their jobs. All those I talked to admit that they started out with a handicap because they did not have a strong enough human-relations background. This does not mean that human relations is the only thing a supervisor must know. There are many special supervisory skills that must be learned. Learning how to delegate, to conduct formal appraisals, to set priorities, to make decisions, and to manage one's time are critical supervisory skills.* If you wish to succeed in a management role, it will be necessary for you to become competent in these areas. You may

---

*The author of this book is also author of *Supervisor's Survival Kit*, fifth ed. (New York: Macmillan Publishing Company, 1990).

wish to study these skills in anticipation of your first supervisory role.

Management training is increasingly demanding. Even if you prepare for and become an excellent supervisor, it is only a start. The more you may aspire to upper-management roles, the more training you should receive. The MBA (master of business administration) graduate degree has become the standard goal of many. Earning an MBA means taking demanding courses in statistics, computer science, management theory, finance, and other areas. If you decide to take this route to the top, keep in mind that in most cases you can earn an MBA while working full time.

If you are intrigued with human relations, it is probably a sign that you will also like management. Although there are many facets to a management job, most involve a great deal of interaction with people. A management job involves counseling, leadership development, and building a competent staff. Some corporate presidents devote over 80 percent of their time to people problems. It is true that an executive manages resources and capital, but the first priority is people management. This will not change.

The discipline factor may not be for you. Those who are not in supervisory roles have the luxury of building rewarding relationships without having to assume the responsibility of correcting the behavior of others. Human relations at the worker level does not involve discipline. Some individuals who are outstanding at human relations are so sensitive to the needs of others and so compassionate in their dealings with others that they cannot correct or discipline those who get out of line. These people are uncomfortable in most leadership roles. They should, therefore, remain workers and make their contribution at that level. Not only will they be unhappy with the constant responsibility to discipline, they will probably not do it well.

Could you make hard decisions? Beginning supervisors must make many decisions each day. The farther up the executive ladder they go, the more critical the decisions become. Most decisions are people decisions. And even those that are primarily productivity or financial decisions affect people.

The fact that you are good at human relations does not necessarily mean you will be good at decision making. In fact, the opposite may be true. For example, a manager may have to make a decision to give a layoff notice to a loyal and competent employee—perhaps even one with whom the manager has an outstanding relationship. There is some indication that the better one is at human relations, the more traumatic such a decision can be. You will want to weigh this factor carefully before deciding to become a supervisor.

Management people are more vulnerable. If you are a highly sensitive person (one reason why you may be good at building positive relationships with others), you may find it difficult to accept the criticism that goes along with a management role. Few, if any, managers are without detractors. In point of fact, whether or not a leader remains a leader often depends upon keeping detractors at a minimum or spotting them soon enough to bring them into the fold.

Do not misunderstand. Your human-relations skills will help you to build good relationships with employees and thus minimize the possibility of negative reactions. You may never have someone under your supervision who becomes so disenchanted that he or she "sets out to get you." But the possibility exists. Despite your own abilities, the role itself makes you more vulnerable. This is in no way intended to keep you from wanting to become supervisor; it simply means that there are disadvantages you should consider in advance.

Your personal attitude is more important—not less! As a supervisor, maintaining your own positive attitude—staying out of attitudinal ruts—is critical. A negative attitude in front of employees is a luxury a person in management cannot afford.

Successful supervisors and leaders at all levels have the ability to create a positive force that pulls employees into a circle of involvement and activity. Once this "force" gets started, it seems to generate confidence among all team members and leads to constructive action and higher productivity.

How do you create a positive force?

Like a pebble dropped into a quiet pool, the power of your positive attitude gets things started. Thus, as a leader, your positive attitude is the *source* of your power. Your positive attitude communicates to those being led that they are headed in a direction that will eventually provide benefits. There are exciting goals within reach. Something better lies over the horizon. A positive attitude in a supervisor/leader builds positive expectations in the minds of workers, whereas a negative attitude destroys them.

The management/leadership challenge is, for many, exciting and rewarding. Those who have taken this career path claim that the challenge has forced them to recognize that their positive attitudes are, indeed, priceless possessions. Now that you have achieved new insights into human behavior and the importance of your own attitude, you are in a better position to decide whether management or leadership roles are for you.

Good luck!

Problem 20

Sensitivity

"I'm chained to my present role."

Bernice is, without question, the most popular and respected employee in the section. She has the rare talent of being able to build meaningful relationships quickly, but she is even better at maintaining them. Her sensitivity to the needs of others is amazing. Co-workers come to her for help on both work-oriented and personal problems, and she seems to have sufficient patience to handle them all.

One fellow employee, however, puts it this way: "Bernice is a pleasure to know and to work with. I sometimes wish she was our supervisor, but I'm afraid the job would chew her up. She is just too nice. It would be difficult, perhaps impossible, for her to get tough and set a firm discipline line. And problem employees would worry her to death."

Bernice is beginning to become bored with her job and is seeking a new challenge. Yesterday, management invited her to become a supervisor of another department.

Assume you are a close friend. Would you recommend that Bernice accept the invitation? (For a suggested answer, see page 197.)

SUGGESTED ANSWERS
TO CASE PROBLEMS

The human-relations problems presented at the end of each chapter in this book are designed to be springboards for individual thinking and discussion purposes. There are no exact answers to any of the problems.

In the first place, only the most essential facts of each problem are outlined. It is therefore impossible to give definite or complete answers to any problem. Without all the facts, anything approaching a definite or complete answer would be dangerous indeed. Also, different points of view are always possible (even encouraged) in discussions of human-relations problems.

The following so-called answers, then, are nothing more than an account of how I would approach the problem with the available facts. They should serve only as a guide to the independent thinking of the reader and the discussion leader.

Problem 1: Reality

It is easy to understand why Rod was disturbed when the other two received promotions ahead of him. His pride was hurt because he had worked hard and efficiently at his job. But there is at least some evidence that Rod was trying to escape his full human-relations responsibility. Did he make enough effort to cooperate and build good relationships with his co-workers, or did he put everything into personal productivity?

The author believes that Rod was not fully justified in saying, "It isn't what know, but who you know, that counts." It appears that Rod was trying to rationalize his unwillingness to build better relationships. He was reminded twice by his supervisor to be more a part of the group. He did not take the hint.

He did not see why he had more of a responsibility to work closely with others in his department in order to help their productivity. Rod's supervisor might have counseled him sooner, more often, and in a more sensitive manner, perhaps citing both good and bad examples from the behavior of others. Rod needs feedback about the specific negative behaviors he demonstrates, the impact they have on others, and some suggested alternatives. The supervisor must assume some of the responsibility for Rod's poor human-relations performance.

Rod's case shows that an ambitious employee who works hard and efficiently does not necessarily make career progress. Rod needs to develop a better balance between productivity and human-relations skills to reach his potential.

Problem 2: Adjustment

George would probably have to make some concessions before he found another job where he would be happy. He failed to understand that when he was aloof and distant he was uncomfortable to work next to. He failed to comprehend that his fellow workers might have needed to communicate with him on a friendly basis, whether he needed to communicate with them or not.

George must learn to relax and give more of himself if he wants an environment in which he can be happy and productive.

He will never make his maximum contribution to his job and company if he stays so deep inside his shell and expects others to come to him.

In discussing the matter with George (as his superior), I would hope to increase his confidence to "come out" and communicate more with others. George does not, as yet, fully sense *why* he should communicate more. I would point out: (1) that it is difficult to work next to a poor communicator (people who act aloof or distant have a way of irritating others) and (2) why such behavior is often misinterpreted (a negative or avoidance response from a person you try to become friendly with can cause you to withdraw). My success with George would depend, in part, upon my skill in getting him to talk more while I am talking less and listening more effectively.

Problem 3: Credit Blues

Although some people can control their consumer credit financing patterns, others seem to get over their heads. They soon struggle to keep up with the interest charges on their statements in addition to making payments on principal amounts. This may have happened to Manuel. When this occurs, a drastic cutback in living standards is often dictated. Only a few people seem to go through such an experience without it having a negative impact on their attitude. Their academic goals and careers are often permanently derailed.

Some suggestions for Manuel include the following:

1. Curtail consumer spending immediately. If necessary destroy your credit cards.

2. Seek less expensive forms of recreation.

3. Accept financial guidance from an expert.

4. Prepare and follow a monthly budget.

5. Anticipate a slow recovery.

Once Manuel is able to see a light at the end of his financial tunnel, his boss and co-workers will probably notice an improvement in his attitude, and his career will be back on track. Manuel might have learned that his positive attitude could be his most priceless possession.

Problem 4: Decision

It is a smart strategy for Bernie to concentrate on building good horizontal relationships—but not to the point that he ignores any opportunity to build a relationship with his aloof boss. Even though his supervisor may appear to be unapproachable, Bernie should continue to wait and watch for opportunities to build a stronger individual relationship through hard work, friendliness, suggestions for improvements, and other means. Just because others have failed to build a healthy relationship with the supervisor doesn't mean that Bernie should give up. He could easily make the mistake of putting all of his human-relations eggs in one horizontal basket.

Problem 5: Message

I go along with the decision to pass Jeff over for the supervisory position, for the following reasons.

1. It would be natural for Jeff's co-workers to resent him as a supervisor. He failed to build good horizontal working relationships with them when he had the chance. Productivity, under his leadership, could drop substantially.

2. An individual who doesn't learn how to build good horizontal relationships as an employee will probably have trouble building good vertical relationships as a supervisor. By neglecting his horizontal working relationships when he first joined the department, Jeff made a classic human-relations mistake.

3. A supervisor achieves more departmental productivity by building good relationships than from the work he actually performs. Jeff would be a poor risk as a supervisor.

Jeff's supervisor should have counseled him more and pointed out other examples of how high producers were passed over at promotion time. He should have explained the relationship between human relations and productivity when he first recognized that Jeff had a problem; that might have enabled Jeff to understand "the big picture." Jeff would thus have had a fair chance to correct his human-relations problem and ready himself for the next supervisory position opportunity.

Problem 6: Insight

Ted's impatience and exasperation are understandable. But the supervisor had a point and was right in counseling him to keep his cool and not further damage his horizontal relationships. Ted was well along the way to becoming a supervisor. If he had continued being critical of others, he might have forfeited his opportunity.

It should be pointed out, however, that Ted was in a tough spot. Due to jealousy and other conflict-causing human factors, it is a human-relations challenge to maintain a personal productivity level above that of your co-workers and still keep good relations with them. However, if Ted really wanted to be the next supervisor, this was the price he might have to pay.

The supervisor was wrong in not giving Ted the "human-relations story" before he became frustrated and damaged his horizontal relationships. Ted must learn, however, that few supervisors are perfect, and that he must protect his future by being human-relations sensitive even when his supervisor is not.

Problem 7: Choice

You have a difficult choice. The older, Theory X supervisor might give you the following advantages: (1) he has been with the company longer and has had more experience, so he might be able to teach you more; and (2) although he may demand more from you, in the long run you might be a stronger person and eventually a better supervisor yourself because of it.

If you choose the younger, Theory Y supervisor, you might enjoy the following advantages: (1) you would probably become more involved under her leadership and, as a result, more productive; and (2) this supervisor would probably move up the management ladder sooner. If you work hard you might be able to take her place and move even higher later on because of her influence from above.

In answering the problem, consider the following:

1. In which work environment would you be most motivated and productive?

2. How would your personality and your values make it with each supervisor?

3. How ambitious are you to get into management?

If you fully understand the leadership styles of each of the two supervisors, you should be able to make the best decision. If you are adaptable, though, neither environment should hurt your personal progress.

Problem 8: Currency

When money is the only currency one deals with, in the long run he or she is apt to be shortchanged. The author would side with Ralph and build a case in the discussion that those who select careers in harmony with their values often come out ahead with money, too, because they build stronger human ties and remain more positive. Those who stay true to their values often enhance their leadership qualities (they gain more respect from followers) and, as a result, qualify for higher-paying positions. There is no documented evidence that those who deal only in the currency of money wind up with more of it.

Problem 9: Frustration

Although company managers were at fault for not having better communications with Vic regarding his future role, it would be difficult to justify such an outburst. What could Vic have done to prevent it? Vic should have investigated the situation more both before he accepted the move and after he arrived at the new plant. In failing to do this, he caused some of his own frustration. Also, if he had been sufficiently aware of his increasing inner tensions, he might have been able to release them off the job—by working in his yard, playing golf, or taking part in some other physical activity that would better suit his style.

It is doubtful whether Vic had seriously hurt his career at this point. It, of course, would depend on the officer who was on the receiving end of the outburst. If he were aware of management's poor communication to Vic or the frustration-aggression idea, he could have easily appreciated Vic's behavior and not made a negative judgment against him.

To play it safe, Vic should have done everything possible to repair (Chapter 10) and strengthen his relationship with the superior officer. If he felt an apology were in order, he should have offered it. He would have benefited from his experience substantially if it taught him to watch for inner signals of tension. That way, he could divert any aggressive behavior into less harmful channels.

Problem 10: Restoration

It is always possible to restore or rebuild a damaged relationship, but Mr. Sisco will need to draw heavily upon his human-relations skills to put this one back together. Some "give" by Dennis also appears necessary. Although either party could initiate the process, Mr. Sisco is the superior and in the better position to take the first step. The author recommends an MRT counseling approach in which an open discussion of differences and "mutual rewards" can take place. Both parties may come to the realization that repairing the break is the only way for each one to come out ahead, from a career point of view. If so, adjustments and renewed communications may follow.

Also, Mr. Sisco is probably resentful about having Dennis "forced" upon him after being asked to find and train a replacement himself. Therefore, Mr. Sisco should initiate a discussion with his own boss(es) to clear the air as well. He should recognize that an unwillingness or inability to prepare Dennis properly to replace him may delay his opportunity to advance, as upper-level managers may begin to question their original presumptions about their selection of Mr. Sisco for promotion.

Problem 11: Nonprofessional

Helen is in a delicate position. The behavior of Thomas in apparently plagiarizing Helen's ideas would be considered "unprofessional," if not "unethical" by most people. But, if she blows the whistle on Thomas without written proof, her accusation could be interpreted by management as "sour grapes" and her own image could be damaged. Although Helen might be tempted to confront Thomas with the matter in front of others, she should resist. This solution could irritate and embarrass Thomas, causing him to go underground and perhaps hurt Helen at a later date. It could also make Helen look bad to co-workers. Helen could, however, confront Thomas in private, so that he knows what he will be up against in the future. She could also protect her creative ideas in the future by refusing to discuss them informally in advance and by submitting them in writing after the idea has been fully developed.

"Openness" is a vital part of human relations. Devious co-workers often destroy the element of trust that is vital in any long-term relationship. The reader is encouraged to isolate and learn from other examples of nonprofessional behavior.

Problem 12: Confrontation

Jane did the right thing under the circumstances. After two months she had had sufficient time to discover that the cause of Ms. Robertson's critical attitude was deep-seated and that time alone would probably not solve the problem. Jane took time to investigate and gather some facts. She discovered, among other things, that two former employees in her position resigned because of Ms. Robertson and her attitude. In other words, this was not surface teasing or testing.

Although Jane took a serious human-relations risk by standing up to Ms. Robertson, she had at least a fair chance of resolving the problem and helping her future. If successful, everybody would come out ahead, including the company and Ms. Robertson.

The reader may not fully agree with the way Jane approached Ms. Robertson or the way in which she expressed herself. To some it may appear that she was too direct and forceful. To others she may have appeared to be overly apologetic. Everyone must go about confrontations of this nature in her (or his) own individual manner. But the principle remains that the cards must often be laid on the table if a sound working relationship is to be created or restored.

As a supervisor, I would initiate a three-way counseling session to air differences openly. Then I would introduce the MRT concept and suggest that Ms. Robertson and Jane try to find a few mutual rewards that might help them build a positive relationship. I would then follow through by complimenting both parties on any progress made, in the hope that such recognition would encourage them to continue to make a strong effort to build a sound relationship.

Problem 13: Balance

Lorraine's absenteeism is getting out of hand and could be called chronic. Her firm could go a reasonable distance to help her learn *how* to do a better job of balancing home and career (Chapter 11). This could be accomplished through a series of counseling sessions or her attendance in a seminar dealing with the subject. Lorraine needs to see the negative impact of her sporadic absenteeism upon company productivity and co-worker relationships. Once this has been achieved, it would be advisable for Lorraine to identify what she can do to reduce her absenteeism. When an employee "owns" the problem, he or she must do the problem solving. This will preserve self-esteem and maintain a healthy manager/employee relationship. With such an attitude, Lorraine and her supervisor should have no trouble working out an "action plan" that everyone can live with. They also need to agree on a time period that will allow Lorraine to bring her absenteeism under control. To start with, she must begin by calling in to her boss each and every time she needs to be absent. Being certain she is truthful every time she gives a "reason" for her absence will also help Lorraine build both her credibility and her self-discipline, presuming she values her job and wishes to remain employed there.

If such efforts do not bring positive results, the firm would be justified to start termination procedures according to personnel policy and legal restrictions. One employee cannot be permitted to drag down departmental productivity over an extended period of time.

Problem 14: Motivation

Berry seems to be out of tune with the modern, high-tempo workplace. He seems to be operating on the ultra-simplistic premise that management has the sole responsibility to motivate employees. Perhaps this comes from Berry's past, where he leaned too heavily on his parents, teachers, and mentors for motivation.

First, Berry must be willing to *listen* to his supervisor and other seasoned employees, while learning to not underestimate them. They apparently have Berry's best interests at heart and want him to succeed. He will need also to consider the principle of openly admitting his mistake (that he "may not have been trying as hard as he could") to his supervisor. As a new employee, his supervisor will most likely give Berry another chance to perform at his competence level. On his own, Berry also needs to start associating with some ambitious co-workers who are scrambling for better roles and greater effectiveness in the workplace. He will soon discover the depth of their self-motivation and whether he is interested in applying his exceptional skills and competencies to become competitive and demonstrate commitment to his job and the organization.

Problem 15: Dilemma

Sylvia made two mistakes. First, she accepted as fact a comment that was not authenticated and could easily have been a rumor. Her second mistake was more serious than the first: she permitted the possible rumor to disturb her emotionally, to the point where it noticeably hurt her productivity.

The facts were not presented in the case, but it is quite possible that the real reason Mr. Young was made department head instead of Sylvia was because Sylvia's efficiency on the job had dropped to the level where management decided to pass her over. If this was what happened, Sylvia permitted a simple rumor to do the greatest possible damage to her future.

Problem 16: Preference

Angelo has an intriguing, but difficult decision ahead of him. In making it he should take a long look at himself and the direction he desires his career path to take. How important is immediate monetary success versus long-range security to him? What are his long-term goals? If Angelo becomes impatient and frustrated over slow, but steady, progress, he should think twice about joining a company that has modest growth potential and makes a practice of promoting from within. The zigzag route to the top might be best.

On the other hand, if Angelo is comfortable with slower, but more secure growth, Company B may be his better bet. Company B may provide more and better training, will perhaps encourage him to finish college at night at its expense, and offer a more comprehensive benefit package. Of course all of this depends upon the future stability of the company. Even firms with strong PFW policies must sometimes go through reorganizations, consolidations, and layoffs.

If Angelo is seeking more immediate upward mobility and he is willing to take the higher risks involved, Company A may be his better bet. Company A may push more responsibility his way sooner. He should keep in mind that he may have to train himself more, and there is always the possibility that he may need to scramble to another company.

Problem 17: Change

Both Jane and Darlene may be successful in adjusting to the dynamic changes of the future, but Darlene appears to be more realistic. When change hits in most organizations, it is not business as usual and most employees can benefit from a new approach.

Darlene is to be applauded for her philosophy of trying to turn change into opportunity, but "looking out for #1" often has a devious connotation that implies a departure from normal ethical and sound human-relations principles to get ahead. If this is Darlene's strategy, her efforts could prove to be counterproductive because she could injure relationships that might provide support she could need at a later date.

Perhaps a combination of maintaining high productivity and sound human relations (Jane) with a creative approach to turning change into opportunity (Darlene) is the best approach. It should also be added that education is the best possible preparation for adapting to change.

Problem 18: Interview

I would accept the following answers as models.

1. "In doing my pre-interview investigation, I discovered that you have an ambitious expansion program and that you have an excellent reputation within the industry for treating people fairly. These features appeal to me."

2. "I will bring my present professional sales skills with me — I feel competent in organizing client data; in my ability to close sales; and about handling rejection — and I would develop other skills such as handling objections on your product line. My goal would be to reach a role where my leadership would help build a stronger organization through teamwork and a balanced emphasis on productivity and sales."

3. "I have concentrated on developing my human-relations competencies. I can build good relations with co-workers and superiors. When I make a mistake, I can repair a relationship. I have received compliments for my skills in problem solving. I am also sensitive to the needs of others. I am a good listener, I understand the positive associations between high productivity and good human relations — especially where clients are concerned."

4. "I reached a plateau in my present company two years ago. Since then I have not been able to take a significant step upward. I believe the main reason is that the company is in a period of reorganization and retrenchment. However, because I was young when I joined them, I made some mistakes. I have learned a great deal since then, and I think I am ready to take full advantage of a fresh start."

5. "I have trouble maintaining my enthusiasm over a long period of time and I tend to scatter my energy in too many directions. I'm working to make improvements in both areas."

Problem 19: Focus

All of the adjustment techniques could help both Lupe and Jack, providing they *recognize* that they are in an attitudinal rut and need a major renewal program. Lupe might benefit most from revitalizing her attitude by giving it away to others (adjustment 3) and looking better to herself (adjustment 4). Jack might benefit most from the flip-side technique (adjustment 1) and placing more emphasis on his "winners" (adjustment 2).

It is, however, most difficult for an outsider to designate any specific adjustment for another individual. Lupe and Jack could experiment with *all* the techniques and then concentrate on those that help the most.

Problem 20: Sensitivity

I would suggest that Bernice stay where she is until she completes a formal course in supervision, after which she would be in a better position to consider the demands of such a job in light of her own personality, values, and goals. It is quite possible that Bernice would agonize so deeply over making hard people decisions that she would render herself ineffective as a supervisor. Not everyone who is highly effective at human relations should become a supervisor. I have known people who were exceptionally competent at working with people at the nonmanagement level but who failed completely in a leadership role. In this respect, it would appear that management may have made a mistake in inviting Bernice to become a supervisor at this early stage. They may be trading their best producer for a supervisor who won't be happy and may leave the organization. This would be a loss to all concerned. On the other hand, with time and experience, people change, mature, and need new challenges. A successful management career is not out of the question for Bernice.

INDEX

Absenteeism
    acceptable reasons, 117
    causes, 119
    company policy, 121
Accepting the physical connection
    (technique), 176
Age and human relations, 76–77
Aggressive behavior. *See also*
    Frustration–aggression
    hypothesis
    appropriate, 82–83
    inappropriate, 83
    recognition of, 84
    types, 85–86
Attitude
    antidote to stress, 168
    definition, 20
    positive, 151
    protecting, 163
    relationship to personality, 15
    renewal, 167
    restoration, 89–94
    serendipitous, 25
    service, 55
    travel, 4
Attitude adjustment scale,
    169
Attitude adjustment techniques,
    172–176

Body language, 105
Bonding, 70

Career
    balancing with home, 99
Charisma, 15
Climates, working, 59
    democratic, 61
    permissive, 60
    structured, 62
    Theory X, Theory Y, Theory Z,
    62

Communications
    forms of, 19
    grapevine, 136–137
    lifeblood comparison, 35
    listening, 124–127
    rumors, 136–137
    verbal and nonverbal signals, 105
Confidence triangle, 140

Discipline line, 62

Employee, new, 99–106
    tips for success, 99–106
Ethnic implications and human
    relations, 61, 68, 129–130

Figure, 8, 95
Flipside (technique), 170
Frustration
    definition, 81
    alleviating, 83
Frustration–aggression hypothesis,
    81
Funny focus, 171–172

Giving your positive attitude to
    others (technique), 173
Grapevine
    definition, 136
    responding to, 137–138

Human relations
    age and, 76–77
    career planning and, 143
    confidence and, 10
    definition, 3
    education and, 14, 102
    importance of, 12
    new employees and, 99–106
    personality and, 15
    preparing for supervisor positions,
    178–183

Human relations (continued)
   productivity and, 5, 45–47
   releasing frustrations, 81–87

Irritation threshold, 78

Leader, becoming one, 175
Leadership style, 63
Life styles. See Value conflicts
Listening, 124
Looking Better to Yourself
   (technique), 174

Management/managers. See
   Supervisors
Management/leadership challenge,
   178–183
Mentors, 65
Mistakes, admitting, 129
Motivation, 130
Mutual reward theory (MRT), 69

Personality conflicts, 130–132, 160.
   See also Teasing; Testing
Playing your winners (technique), 172
Plateau periods
   coping with, 153–155
   definition, 151
   Plan B, 144–149
   reasons for, 152
Productivity
   definition, 7
   group (departmental), 41–45
   individual (personal), 41
   levels of, 41
   measuring, 40
Productivity gaps, 42
Promotion from within (PFW), 143.
   See also Stabilizers

Relationships
   characteristics, 68–77
   definition, 31
   frustrations with, 81–87
   restoring injured, 89–94
   underestimating others, 127
Relationships, horizontal
   definition, 36
   examples, 37

importance of, 37–38
   responsibility for, 36
Relationships, vertical
   definition, 34
   examples, 34
   importance of, 34–38
   responsibility for, 35
Resignation
   appropriate ways, 158–161
   considerations, 159–161
   dangers of, 158
Rumors
   definition, 135
   responding to, 136–137

Scramblers
   advantages, 146
   definition, 143
   disadvantages, 147
   plateau periods and, 151–155
Sexual overtones and human
   relations, 74
Signals
   verbal and nonverbal, 105
Stabilizers
   advantages, 145
   definition, 143
   disadvantages, 145
Stress and attitude, 168
Success, tips for, 99–106
Supervisors
   human relations foundation,
      178–179
   preparation for, 180
   working climates, 43, 148
Symbiotic relationship, 14

Teasing, 108–110
Testing
   coping with, 111
   organizational, 110
   personal, 110–112
Tolerance level, 78

Underestimating others, 124

Value conflicts and human relations,
   71
Victimizing yourself, 130–132